KOREAN GRAMMAR for Beginners

I0458539

LEARN Korean

GRAMMAR WORKBOOK FOR BEGINNERS

- ☑ Master Essential Korean Grammar Patterns Step-by-Step
- ☑ Practice with Targeted Writing Exercises & Quizzes
- ☑ Clear Explanations with Everyday Korean Examples
- ☑ Conversation Tips to Use Grammar Confidently
- ☑ Consistent Progress from Basics to Fluency

한국어를 배우다 입문서

POLYSCHOLAR

www.polyscholar.com

CONTENTS

Scan the QR code or click on the link below to receive all the exercises from this book in a printable PDF. That way you can practice as much as you like.

https://go.polyscholar.com/kgb

Introduction

Welcome to **"Learn Korean for Beginners: Grammar and Language Essentials"**, your guide to embarking on a journey into the Korean language with confidence and enthusiasm! This book is designed to help you take your first steps toward mastering Korean, focusing on foundational elements that make learning both enjoyable and rewarding. Whether you are learning for travel, work, cultural interest, or just a love for the language, this book will guide you through everything you need to start expressing yourself in Korean. What's Inside This Book?

What's Inside This Book?

This book is structured into 30 chapters, each crafted to introduce new vocabulary, essential grammar patterns, and practical conversation skills. Here's what each chapter offers:

• **Vocabulary:** Carefully selected words around key themes (like family, food, hobbies, and daily routines) to build a practical foundation.

• **Conversation Practice:** Real-life scenarios and dialogues to put vocabulary in context and show how words and phrases flow naturally in Korean conversations.

• **Grammar Patterns:** Three essential patterns per chapter, explained in an accessible way to help you construct sentences, ask questions, and express yourself accurately.

• **Exercises:** Engaging activities to reinforce what you've learned, giving you the confidence to make the language your own.

How This Book Can Help You

Learning Korean isn't just about language—it's a gateway to understanding Korean culture, history, and the unique perspectives embedded in its . language. Hangeul, Korea's phonetic alphabet, was crafted to be logical and accessible, allowing you to dive into Korean quickly and begin using it in everyday situations. With each chapter building progressively on the last, this book gives you a clear and supportive pathway to develop foundational skills.

Why Learn Korean?

Korean offers you direct access to popular culture, from K-dramas and K-pop to literature and food, and opens doors to meaningful interactions with native speakers. By mastering basic vocabulary and grammar, you can start appreciating Korean not only as a language but as a unique form of expression with deep cultural roots.

So, open up to Chapter 1, and let's embark on this exciting journey into Korean together. With each lesson, you'll get closer to understanding and experiencing the value and beauty of Korean.

Ready to begin? Let's go!

Preliminary Lesson

I. Korean Script

The Korean script, known as Hangul (한글), was developed in the 15th century during the reign of King Sejong the Great. Before Hangul's creation, Koreans primarily used Classical Chinese characters, which were complex and difficult for the average person to learn. Recognizing the need for a simpler writing system accessible to all, King Sejong initiated the development of Hangul.

The Concept of Sky, Land, and Earth in Hangul

The Hangul script is imbued with symbolic meaning, particularly in its representation of the concepts of sky, land, and earth. This tripartite symbolism reflects the Korean worldview and the philosophical underpinnings of the language.

- **Sky (하늘, Haneul):** Represented by the vowel ㅏ (a), symbolises aspirations and the divine connection.
- **Land (땅, ttang):** Represented by the vowel ㅗ (o), signifies stability and the nurturing aspect of nature, representing community roots.
- **Earth (지구, Jigu):** Represented by the consonant ㅇ (ng), symbolises the material world and interconnectedness of all living beings.

Concept	Hangul Symbol	Symbolism
Sky	ㅏ	*Elevation and aspirations*
Land	ㅗ	*Stability and community roots*
Earth	ㅇ	*Material reality and harmony*

II. Introduction to Korean Pronunciation

Hangul, the Korean writing system, is unique not only for its design but also for its phonetic nature, making it relatively straightforward to pronounce once the basic rules are understood. In this lesson, we will explore how to pronounce Hangul letters, including consonants and vowels, and provide examples to facilitate learning.

1. Basic Components of Hangul

Hangul consists of 14 basic consonants and 10 basic vowels. Each letter has a specific sound, and when combined, they form syllables.

A. Consonants

Here are the basic consonants and their pronunciation:

Hangul	Romanization	Pronunciation
ㄱ	g/k	Between "g" and "k"
ㄴ	n	"n" as in "no"
ㄷ	d/t	Between "d" and "t"
ㄹ	r/l	"r" (light) or "l"
ㅁ	m	"m" as in "mom"
ㅂ	b/p	Between "b" and "p"
ㅅ	s	"s" as in "see"
ㅇ	ng	Silent at start / "ng"
ㅈ	j	"j" as in "jazz"

ㅊ	ch	"ch" as in "chat"
ㅋ	k	"k" as in "kite"
ㅌ	t	"t" as in "top"
ㅍ	p	"p" as in "pop"
ㅎ	h	"h" as in "hat"

B. Vowels

Here are the basic vowels and their pronunciation:

Hangul	Romanization	Pronunciation
ㅏ	a	"**a**" as in "father"
ㅑ	ya	"ya" as in "yarn"
ㅓ	eo	"uh" as in "sun"
ㅕ	yeo	"yuh" as in "young"
ㅗ	o	"o" as in "go"
ㅛ	yo	"yo" as in "yoga"
ㅜ	u	"oo" as in "moon"
ㅠ	yu	"yu" as in "yule"
ㅡ	eu	"eu" as in "put" (with rounded lips)
ㅣ	i	"ee" as in "see"

C. Compound Consonants

Compound consonants are tense or "doubled" versions of basic consonants, pronounced with more force and no air release. They create a sharper, more intense sound compared to their basic forms.

Hangul	Romanization	Pronunciation
ㄲ	*kk*	Hard "k" (tense)
ㄸ	*tt*	Hard "t" (tense)
ㅃ	*pp*	Hard "p" (tense)
ㅆ	*ss*	Hard "s" (tense)
ㅉ	*jj*	Hard "j" (tense)

D. Compound Vowels

Compound vowels are formed by combining two basic vowels, creating blended sounds. These are used to represent diphthongs, where two vowel sounds are merged into a single syllable.

Hangul	Romanization	Pronunciation
ㅐ	*ae*	"e" as in "bad"
ㅒ	*yae*	"yae" as in "yeah"
ㅔ	*e*	"e" as in "get"
ㅖ	*ye*	"ye" as in "yes"
ㅘ	*wa*	"wa" as in "water"
ㅙ	*wae*	"wae" as in "way"

괴	*oe*	"oe" as in "wag"
궈	*wo*	"wo" as in "wonder"
궤	*we*	"we" as in "wet"
귀	*wi*	"wi" as in "week"
긔	*ui*	"ui" as in "oui" (French)

2. Combining Consonants and Vowels

In Hangul, consonants and vowels combine to form syllables. A syllable block typically consists of an initial consonant, a vowel, and sometimes a final consonant.

Example

- 가 (**ga**): ㄱ + ㅏ
- 마 (**ma**): ㅁ + ㅏ
- 한 (**han**): ㅎ + ㅏ + ㄴ
- 봄 (**bom**): ㅂ + ㅗ + ㅁ

3. Pronunciation Tips

- **Initial Position:** Consonants are pronounced more forcefully when they occur at the beginning of a syllable.
- **Final Position:** Some consonants sound slightly different when at the end of a syllable. For example, ㄱ sounds like a soft g.
- **Nasal Sounds:** The final consonant ㅇ creates a nasal sound and often indicates the end of a syllable without adding an extra vowel sound.

III. Korean Sentence Structure

Korean sentences consist of either "a subject + predicate (verb)"
Or " a subject + object + predicate (verb).

지수 + 가 + 자요. (Jisoo sleeps)
Subject   predicate

지민이가 + 밥을 + 먹어요. (Jimin is eating rice)
Subject   object   predicate

Particles are attached to words in Korean sentences.
- After the subject, 이 or 가 is used.
- After an object, the particle을 or 를 is used.
- After an adverbial, 에 or 에게 is used.

i. 지원이가 사과를 먹어요. **(Jiwon eats an apple)**
   Subject   Object   Verb

ii. 민석이가 책을 도서관에서 읽어요. **(Minseok reads a book in the library.)**
   Subject adverb   object   predicate

Predicates always come at the very end of the sentence, the order of
subjects, objects and adverbial changes depending on the intention
of the speaker.

iii. 사과를 + 지원이가 + 먹어요. **(Jiwon eats an apple)**
   object   Subject   predicate

iv. 책을 + 도서관에서 + 민석이가 + 읽어요. **(Minseok reads book in the library.)**
   object   adverb   subject   verb

In addition, when the subject can be clearly understood from the context, it can be omitted.

가: 지원이가 뭐 해요?   What is Jiwon doing?
나: 사과를 먹어요.   Eating apple.
(we omitted Jiwon here, because it is clearly understood from the context that we're talking about Jiwon).

가: 어디에 가요?   Where are you going?
나: 학교에 가요.   I am going to school.
(As we can see here, that we omitted you and I in Korean sentences because it is clear that someone is talking to the person, who is in front of him or her).

IV. Korean Conjugation Basics

1. Introduction

Korean verbs and adjectives are conjugated according to the following reasons.

- Tense
- Politeness level
- Passive
- Causative forms
- Speech style

2. Conjugating Verbs

In Korean, verbs are always conjugated at the end of a sentence. The base form of a verb ends in -다 (e.g., 가다, 먹다). When you conjugate, you remove the -다 and add the appropriate ending.

A. Present Tense

For the present tense, conjugation depends on whether the verb stem ends in a vowel or consonant.

Vowel-ending stems: Add -아요 (if the last vowel is ㅏ or ㅗ) or -어요 (for other vowels).

가다 (to go) → 가요 (I go)
보다 (to see) → 봐요 (I see)

Consonant-ending stems: Add -아요 or -어요 as well.

먹다 (to eat) → 먹어요 (I eat)
읽다 (to read) → 읽어요 (I read)

B. Past Tense

The past tense is formed by adding -았어요 (for stems with ㅏ or ㅗ) or -었어요 (for other stems).

가다 → 깄어요 (I went)
먹다 → 먹었어요 (I ate)
공부하다 (to study) → 공부했어요 (I studied)

C. Future Tense

For the future tense, add -을 거예요 for consonant-ending stems or -ㄹ 거예요 for vowel-ending stems.

가다 → 갈 거예요 (I will go)
먹다 → 먹을 거예요 (I will eat)

4. Conjugating Adverb

Korean adjectives function similarly to verbs. They also change forms based on tense and politeness. Adjectives end in -다 in their base form.

A. Present Tense

Just like verbs, adjectives conjugate using -아요 or -어요 depending on the last vowel.

크다 (to be big) → 커요 (It's big)
작다 (to be small) → 작아요 (It's small)

B. Past Tense

To express past tense, you add -았어요 or -었어요, following the same rule.

크다 (to be big) → 컸어요 (It was big)
작다 (to be small) → 작았어요 (It was small)

5. Politeness Level

Korean has different politeness levels, which change how verbs and adjectives are conjugated. We've seen the polite style (ending in -요) so far. Here's a brief overview of other common styles:

Informal: Drop the ㅡ다.
가다 → 가 (Go)
먹다 → 먹어 (Eat)

Formal: Add -습니다 **or** -ㅂ니다.
가다 → 갑니다 **(I go)**
먹다 → 먹습니다 **(I eat)**

Polite: Add the ㅡ요.
가다 → 가요. (Go)
먹다 → 먹어요. (Eat)

Summary of Key Differences:

Tense	Informal	Polite	Formal
Present	자	자요	잡니다
	사	사요	삽니다
Past	잤어	잤어요	잤습니다
	샀어	샀어요	샀습니다
Future	잘 거야	잘 거예요	잘 것입니다
	살 거야	살 거예요	살 것입니다

Chapter- 1
INTRODUCING YOURSELF

I. Vocabulary

나	I
저	I (저 is the polite equivalent of 나)
여러분	Ladies and gentleman
씨	Mr./ Ms.
선생님	Teacher
학생	Student
회사원	Employee
가수	Singer
배우	Actor/ Actress
학교	School
회사	Company
네	yes
아니요	No
미국	America
영국	United Kingdom
인도	India
인도네시아	Indonesia
대한민국	Republic of Korea
태국	Thailand

중국	China
독일	Germany
일본	Japan
프랑스	France
러시아	Russia
서울대학교	Seoul University
삼성	Samsung

Expressions

실례합니다.	Excuse me
이름이 뭐예요?	What is your name?
처음 뵙겠습니다.	Literally means "I am meeting you for the first time"
만나서 반갑습니다.	Literally means "I am glad we met" (Can be used any time you meet someone)

II. Conversation

가: 처음 뵙겠습니다.	Nice to meet you for the first time.
나: 네, 처음 뵙겠습니다.	Yes, nice to meet you for the first time.
가: 저는 김민준입니다.	I am Kim Minjun.
이름이 뭐예요?	What is your name?
나: 저는 박지민입니다.	My name is Park Jimin.
가: 만나서 반갑습니다.	Nice to meet you.
나: 네, 만나서 반갑습니다.	Nice to meet you too.

Note: 가 means he/she and 나 means I or me. Please refer to this for future conversations.

III. Grammar

1. Topic Marker: (은/는)

The topic marker 은/는 is used to introduce the topic of the sentence, giving information about what the sentence is about or to contrast with something previously mentioned. It doesn't necessarily emphasise the subject itself but provides a general context for what will be talked about.

How to Use 은/는:

- Use 은 after a noun that ends in a consonant.
- Use 는 after a noun that ends in a vowel.

Examples:

- 책(Book)＋ 은 ＝책은
- 친구(Friend)＋ 는＝ 친구는
- 저는 학생입니다.
- 잭슨은 가수입니다.

2. Formal Statements: ~입니다

~입니다 is a polite and formal ending used in declarative sentences to express facts, introduce oneself, or describe things. It is the equivalent of "is/am/are" in English, but it is used at the end of the sentence to maintain the typical Korean subject-object-verb structure.

How to Use ~입니다

Attach 입니다 to a noun to create a polite formal statement. 입니다 is essential in formal or respectful settings, such as when introducing yourself, presenting facts, or giving formal explanations.

Examples:

   i. 가: 저는 투안입니다.
     나: 저는 사쿠라입니다.
  ii. 가: 저는 태국 사람입니다.
     나: 저는 일본 사람입니다.
 iii. 저는 회사원입니다.

Note: 사람 means 'human' or 'person', when you want to introduce the country you're from or someone from, you can add 사람 to the country's name to denote nationality. For Eg., 일본 + 사람 = 일본 사람.

                          Japan Person Japanese

3. Formal Questions: ~입니까?

입니까? is the formal and polite ending used to ask questions. It is used in place of 입니다 when you need to inquire or confirm information.

How to Use ~입니까?

Attach 입니까? to a noun to form a question.

     학생입니까? → "Are you a student?"

Like 입니다, 입니까? is essential for maintaining a respectful tone, especially in formal settings or when speaking to strangers, elders, or superiors.

Examples:

i. 가: 학생입니까?
　　나: 네, 학생입니다.
ii. 가: 민수씨는 가수입니까?
　　나: 아니요, 회사원입니다.
iii. 사냄씨는 배우입니까?
　　나: 네, 배우입니다.

IV. Exercise

1. Fill in the Blanks (Subject Particles: 는/은)

i. 저＿＿＿＿ 학생입니다.

ii. 선생님＿＿＿＿ 한국 사람입니다.

iii. 잭슨씨＿＿＿＿ 중국 사람입니다.

iv. 이 분 ＿＿＿＿ 가수입니다.

v. 이 배우 ＿＿＿＿ 미국사람입니다.

2. Complete the Dialogue by using vocabulary.

i. A: 실례합니다. ＿＿＿＿＿＿＿.

　 B: 네, ＿＿＿＿＿＿. 제 이름은 태민입니다.

ii. A: 여러분, 이분은 한국 ＿＿＿＿＿＿＿입니다.

　 B: 만나서 ＿＿＿＿＿＿.

iii. A: 저는 ＿＿＿＿＿＿ 사람입니다.

　　 B: 아, 처음 뵙겠습니다. 저는 ＿＿＿＿＿＿입니다.

iv. A: 안녕하세요. 저는 삼성 ＿＿＿＿＿＿입니다.

　　 B: 안녕하세요. 저는 한국대학교 ＿＿＿＿＿＿입니다.

3. Write the Names of the Marked Countries in Korean.

i. _____

ii. _____

iii. _____

iv. _____

v. _____

4. Complete each sentence by choosing the appropriate vocabulary.

i. 저는 _____입니다. (I am a student.)

ii. 안녕하세요. 저는 지민 _____. (Hello, I am Jimin.)

iii. _____. 이름이 뭐예요? (Excuse me, what is your name?)

iv. _____은 배우입니다. (Mr./Ms. Kim is an actor.)

v. 여러분, _____ 반갑습니다.

(Ladies and gentlemen, I am glad to meet you.)

Chapter - 2
EVERYDAY OBJECTS

I. Vocabulary

이것	This
그것	It
저것	That
이	This
그	It
저	That
책	Book
사전	Dictionary
잡지	Magazine
신문	Newspaper
공책	Notebook
명함	Business card
연필	Pencil
볼펜	Ballpoint pen
시계	Clock
우산	Umbrella
책상	Desk
의자	Chair
영어	English
한국어	Korean
일본어	Japanese
무엇, 뭐	What
그래서	So,
그래요?	Is that so?

읽다	to read
보다	to see/watch
공부하다	to study
좋아하다	to like
하다	to do

Expressions

안녕하세요	Hello.
좋은 아침입니다	Good morning
안녕히 가세요	Goodbye (in formal when someone is leaving and you are staying)
안녕히 계세요	Goodbye (in formal when you are leaving and someone is staying)
안녕히 주무세요	Good Night.
감사합니다	Thank You.
잘 부탁드립니다	Please be nice to me. (People often say it to someone they meet for the first time).

II. Conversation

가: 안녕하세요!	Hello!
나: 안녕하세요!	Hello!
가: 이 책이 무엇이에요?	What is this book?
나: 이것은 한국어 사전이에요.	This is a Korean dictionary.
가: 그렇군요!	Oh, I see!
저도* 한국어를 공부해요.	I also study Korean.
나: 정말요?	Really?
저도 한국어를 공부해요.	I also study Korean.
가: 잘 부탁드립니다.	Please be nice to me.

Note: 도 means "also" or "too" and replaces 은/는, 이/가, or 을/를 to add inclusivity. It indicates that something applies to an additional subject or object.

III. Grammar

1. Object Particles: 을 and 를

In Korean, the object of a sentence (the thing that the action is being done to) is marked by 을 or 를. These particles make it clear what is being acted upon in the sentence.

How to Use 을/를:

- 을 is used if the noun ends in a consonant
- 를 is used if the noun ends in a vowel.

Examples:

- 책(Book)＋ 을 ＝책을
- 친구 (Friend)＋ 를＝ 친구를
- 잡지를 읽어요?
- 책을 읽어요.
- 그 사람을 좋아해요.

2. Negative Statements with 안

To make a sentence negative, use 안 before the verb. This is similar to saying "not" in English. 안 is an easy way to make negative statements, and it's commonly used in informal and polite speech.

How to Use 안

The structure is straightforward: place 안 directly before the verb to negate it.

Examples:

- 잡지를 안 읽어요.

Here, 안 is added before 읽어요 (to read) to express that the action of reading is not happening.

- 책을 안 읽어요.

In this example, 안 negates 읽어요, so the sentence means "I don't read a book."

- 그 사람을 안 좋아해요.

In this sentence, 안 is added before 좋아해요 (to like) to negate the action, expressing that the speaker does not like the person.

3. Verb Conjugation: Present Tense~ 아요/ 어요.

In Korean, verbs change form based on tense and politeness level. Here, we're focusing on polite present tense, which is used to express actions happening now or habits you do regularly.

Using the correct present tense endings is crucial for making polite and clear statements in Korean.

How to conjugate verbs into -요 form

- Start with the verb stem (remove 다 from the dictionary form)
- If the verb stem ends in the vowel ㅏ or ㅗ, add 아요.
- If the verb stem ends in any other vowel, add 어요

Dictionary Form	Verb Stem	Last Vowel	Present Tense
읽다	읽	other	읽어요
보다	보	오	봐요
공부하다	공부하	아	공부해요
좋아하다	좋아하	아	좋아해요

Examples:

- 읽다 → 읽어요 (to read becomes I read).
- 보다 → 봐요 (to see becomes I see)
- 공부하다 → 공부해요 (to study becomes I study)
- 좋아하다 → 좋아해요 (to like becomes I like)
- 한국어를 공부해요
- 잡지를 좋아해요

IV. Exercise

1. Fill in the blanks with the correct object particle (을 or 를)

i. 책_____ 읽어요.

ii. 한국어 _____ 공부해요.

iii. 잡지_____ 봐요.

iv. 영화_____ 좋아해요.

v. 연필_____ 사용해요.

2. Conjugate the following verbs into the present tense polite form.

i. 읽다 (to read) → _____

ii. 공부하다 (to study) → _____

iii. 보다 (to see/watch) → _____

iv. 좋아하다 (to like) → _____

v. 하다 (to do) → _____

3. Rewrite the following sentences as negative sentences using 안:

    i. 저는 신문을 읽어요. → _____

    ii. 저는 영어를 공부해요. → _____

    iii. 저는 잡지를 봐요. → _____

    iv. 저는 일을 해요. → _____

    v. 저는 영화를 좋아해요. → _____

4. Match the Korean word with its English meaning:

    i. 책   a. Magazine

    ii. 사전   b. Newspaper

    iii. 잡지   c. Korean language

    iv. 신문   d. Book

    v. 한국어   e. Dictionary

5. Read the given paragraph and answer the following questions:

> 안녕하세요! 저는 잡지를 읽어요. 하지만 신문은 안 읽어요. 저는 한국어도 공부해요. 책을 좋아해요, 그래서 매일 책을 읽어요. 볼펜과 연필도 항상 가지고 있어요. 감사합니다!

i. 저는 무엇을 읽어요?

ii. 저는 신문을 읽어요? 아니면 안 읽어요?

iii. 저는 무엇을 좋아해요?

iv. 저는 한국어를 공부해요? 아니면 공부 안 해요?

v. 저는 무엇을 항상 가지고 있어요?

6. Write a paragraph about your daily life.

Chapter- 3

PLACES AND POSSESSIONS

I. Vocabulary

장소[Place]

여기	Here
거기	There
저기	Over There
어디	Where
회사	Company
사무실	Office
화장실	Restroom
식당	Restaurant
집	House
기숙사	Dormitory
빨래방	Laundromat
미용실	Hair Salon
시장	Markct
마트	Mart
편의점	Convenience store
슈퍼마켓	Supermarket

물건[Objects]

가족 사진	Family Picture
가방	Bag

여권	Passport
거울	Mirror
화장품	Cosmetics
빗	Comb
헤어드라이어	Hair dryer
베개	Pillow
이불	Blanket

Expression

어디예요?	Where are you?
어디 가세요?	Where are you going?
어디서 왔어요?	Where are you from?
미안해요.	I am sorry
이것은 뭐예요?	What is this?

II. Conversation

가:안녕하세요! 어디 가세요? — Hello! Where are you going?
나: 안녕하세요! 회사에 가요. — Hello! I'm going to the company.
가: 제 지갑이 여기에 있어요? — Is my wallet here?
나: 아니요, 지갑이 여기에 없어요. — No, the wallet isn't here.
가: 아, 미안해요. — Ah, sorry.
　　제 가방은 어디에 있어요? — Where is my bag?
나: 가방은 저기 있어요. — The bag is over there.
가: 감사합니다! — Thank you!
　　그리고 이것은 뭐예요? — And what is this?
나: 아, 그거 제 가족 사진이에요. — Oh, that's my family photo.
가: 사진이 예뻐요! — The photo is pretty!
나: 고마워요! — Thank you!

III. Grammar

1. Subject Particle: ~이/가

The subject particles 이/가 attaches to nouns to indicate the subject of the sentence. It is used to highlight the subject in a sentence and is attached according to the final consonant of the noun.

How to Use ~이/가

- 이 follows nouns ending in a consonant.
- 가 follows nouns ending in a vowel.
- When 가 is followed by the noun such as 저, 나, 너 it becomes 제가, 내가, 네가.

Examples

i. 가방이 어디에 있어요?
ii. 가족 사진이 여기에 있어요.
iii. 거울이 화장실에 있어요.
iv. 여기가 기숙사입니까?

2. Location Marker: ~에

The location marker ~에 is used to indicate where something or someone is or where someone is going. It is attached to the place where something exists or is located.

Examples

i. 사무실에 가세요?
ii. 편의점에 가방이 있어요.
iii. 기숙사에 있어요
iv. 잭슨씨가 한국에 있어요

3. Possession Particle ~의

The possession marker ~의 is used to indicate ownership or association. It is similar to "s" in English and connects the owner to the object.

Examples

i. 가족의 집입니다.
ii. 친구의 지갑이에요.
iii. 민수씨의 헤어드라이어입니다.
iv. 그것은 누구의 화장품입니까?

IV. Exercise

1. Fill in the Blanks with the Correct Marker (~이/가, ~에, or ~의):

i. 가방 ___ 어디에 있어요?

ii. 화장실 ___ 저기에 있어요.

iii. 친구 ___ 가족 사진이에요.

iv. 식당 ___ 있어요?

2. Write the correct answer by filling in the blanks with ~에

Example: 가방 ___ 식당 Answer: 가방이 식당에 있어요.

i. 지갑 ___ 사무실

ii. 거울 ___ 화장실

iii. 가족 사진 ___ 집

iv. 이불___빨래방

3. Rearrange the Words to Form a Correct Sentence

Example: Words: 사진 / 가족 / 여기 / 이 / 에 있어요
Correct Sentence:가족 사진이 에 있어요.

i. Words: 가방 / 편의점 / 에 / 있어요 / 가방이

Correct Sentence: _____

ii. Words: 화장실 / 거울 / 에 / 있어요 / 거울이

Correct Sentence: _____

iii. Words: 지갑 / 사무실 / 에 / 있어요 / 지갑이

Correct Sentence: _____

iv. Words: 집 / 이불 / 에 / 있어요 / 이불이

Correct Sentence: _____

4. Choose the Correct Marker (~이/가, ~에, or ~의)

i. _____ 집이에요?

a) 이곳이
b) 이곳에
c) 이곳의
d) 이곳가

ii. 화장실 _____ 거울이 있어요.
   a) 화장실이
   b) 화장실에
   c) 화장실의
   d) 화장실가

iii. 가방 _____ 빨래방에 가요.
   a) 가방이
   b) 가방에
   c) 가방의
   d) 가방가

iv. 식당 _____ 어디예요?
   a) 식당이
   b) 식당에
   c) 식당의
   d) 식당가

5. Match to the corresponding words.

   i.   Cosmetics   a. 베개

   ii. Restaurant   b. 가방

   iii. Pillows   c. 식당

   iv. Mart   d. 집

   v.   House   e. 마트

   vi. Bag   f. 화장품

Chapter- 4

I. Vocabulary

장소[Place]

건물	Building
계단	Stairs
교회	Church
도서관	Library
박물관	Museum
병원	Hospital/ Clinic
우체국	Post office
학원	An Academy
호텔	Hotel
공원	Park
동네	Neighbourhood
카페	A Cafe/ Coffee Shop
PC방	Internet Cafe
은행	Bank
백화점	Department Store

물건[Things]

냉장고	A refrigerator
노트북	A laptop
다리미	An Iron

텔레비전	Television
가구	Furniture
소파	Sofa
책장	A Bookshelf
침대	Bed
피아노	Piano
테이블/탁자	Table
핸드폰/휴대폰	Smart Phone
사진	Photo
식탁	Dining Table
카메라/사진기	Camera

Expression

어떻게 지내세요?	How are you doing?
누구?/누구세요?	Who's that? /Who is it?
잠시만요.	Just a moment, please.
아니요, 안돼요.	No, that's impossible.
네, 좋아요.	OK, it's fine.
맞아요.	That's right.
아마도요.	Perhaps /Maybe.

Abbreviations

이것이= 이게	This
저것이= 저게	That
그것이= 그게	It

II. Conversation

민지: 안녕하세요 지수 씨!
　　　어떻게 지내세요??

지수: 잘 지내요.
　　　민지 씨 오늘 어디에 가요?

민지: 저는 병원에 가요.
　　　민지 씨는요?

지수: 저는 우체국에 가요.
　　　우체국은 동네에 있어요.

민지: 아, 그래요.
　　　우체국에 잘 다녀오세요!

지수: 네, 감사합니다!

Minji: Hello, Jisoo!
How are you?

Jisoo: I'm doing well.
Minji, where are you going today?

Minji: I'm going to the hospital.
What about you?

Jisoo: I'm going to the post office.
The post office is in my neighborhood.

Minji: Oh, I see.
Have a good trip to the post office!

Jisoo: Yes, thank you!

III. Grammar

1. N이에요/예요 [is, am, are (polite form)]

이에요/예요 is the polite way to say "is/am/are" in Korean.
It's used to identify or describe nouns.

- It's the equivalent of **"to be"** in English.

This pattern is often used in everyday conversations and polite speech to describe people, objects, places, and identities.

How to Use 이에요/예요

- **Noun +** 이에요: Attach "이에요" if the noun ends with a consonant.
  - **Example:** 책 + 이에요 → 책이에요 (It's a book).

- **Noun +** 예요: Attach "예요" if the noun ends with a vowel.
  - **Example:** 학교 + 예요 → 학교예요 (It's a school).

Example

- 이것은 냉장고예요.
- 저것은 병원이 아니에요.
- 여기는 공원이에요.
- 저는 학생이에요.
- 저 사람은 선생님이에요.

2. Noun + 에 가다/오다 (Going to/Coming to)

This grammar pattern is used to describe someone's movement to a specific place.

- 에 가다 means "to go to" a place.
- 에 오다 means "to come to" a place.

The particle 에 indicates the destination where the movement is directed.

How to Use N + 에 가다/오다

Noun + 에 가다: Used when indicating that someone is going to a location.

- **Example:** 도서관 + 에 가다 → 도서관에 가요
(I'm going to the library)

Noun + 에 오다: Used when indicating that someone is coming to a location.

- **Example:** 학교 + 에 오다 → 학교에 와요
(I'm coming to school).

Example

- 저는 박물관에 가요.
- 친구가 우리 집에 와요.
- 내일 우체국에 가요.
- 그는 학원에 다녀요.
- 엄마가 시장에 가요.

3. Location Markers: ~에 있다/없다

있다 means "to exist" or "to be present" at a location, while 없다 means "to not exist" or "to not be present" at a location.

The particle 에 indicates the location where someone or something exists or does not exist.

This pattern is used to indicate the presence or absence of people, objects, or things in a particular place.

How to Use ~에 있다/없다

Noun + 에 있다: To indicate that someone or something is at a location.

- Example: 공원 + 에 있다 → 공원에 있어요
  (At the park).

Noun + 에 없다: To indicate that someone or something is not at a location.

- Example: 집 + 에 없다 → 집에 없어요
  (Not at home).

Example

- 아빠는 회사에 있어요.
- 친구가 카페에 없어요.
- 가방은 교실에 있어요.
- 고양이가 방에 있어요.

IV. Exercise

1. Fill in the Blank (N이에요/예요)

  i. 이것은 노트북_____.

  ii. 저 건물은 도서관_____.

  iii. 여기는 공원_____.

  iv. 저 사람은 의사_____.

  v. 이 물건은 냉장고_____.

2. Form sentences using the given words and the grammar patterns you've learned.

  i. 냉장고 / 거실 / 있다

  ii. 친구 / 공원 / 가다

  iii. 선생님 / 학교 / 없다

  iv. 동생 / 도서관 / 오다

  v. 사진 / 벽 / 있다

3. Choose the correct word to complete the sentence.

i. 저는 내일 _____에 갈 거예요.

a) 사진

b) 병원

c) 핸드폰

ii. 동생이 _____에서 피아노를 연습해요.

a) 학원

b) 우체국

c) 책장

iii. 아버지는 _____에 있어요.

a) 계단

b) 은행

c) 다리미

iv. 우리는 주말에 _____에 가요.

a) 공원

b) 노트북

c) 침대

v. 이곳은 _____이에요/예요.

a) 카메라

b) 테이블

c) 교회

4. Answer the following questions using 이에요 or 예요.

    i. 이것은 무엇이에요? (카메라)

    ii. 저 사람은 누구예요? (선생님)

    iii. 저 건물은 무엇이에요? (도서관)

    iv. 이 물건은 무엇이에요? (텔레비전)

    v. 이곳은 어디예요? (은행)

5. Read the passage and answer the following questions:

미나는 아침에 도서관에 가요. 도서관에는 많은 책이 있어요. 미나는 책을 읽고, 노트북으로 공부도 해요. 점심 시간에 미나는 카페에 가서 커피를 마셔요. 그 후에 친구와 함께 공원에 가요. 공원에는 사람들이 많이 있어요. 미나는 저녁에 집에 와요. 집에는 침대와 소파가 있어요.

i. 미나는 아침에 어디에 가요?

a) 병원

b) 도서관

c) 학원

ii. 도서관에 무엇이 있어요?

a) 가방

b) 사진

c) 책

iii. 미나는 점심 시간에 어디에 가요?

a) 우체국

b) 카페

c) 호텔

iv. 공원에 사람들이 있어요?

a) 네, 있어요.

b) 아니요, 없어요.

v. 미나는 저녁에 집에 와요?

a) 맞아요

b) 아니요

vi. 미나의 집에는 무엇이 있어요?

Chapter- 5
TIME AND SCHEDULE

I. Vocabulary

가다	to go
오다	to come
돌아가다/돌아오다	to return
학교	school
슈퍼마켓	supermarket
역	station
비행기	airplane
배	ship/ boat
기차	train
지하철	subway
버스	bus
택시	taxi
사람	person, people
친구	friend
남자	man
여자	woman
가족	family
혼자	alone, by oneself

지난주	last week
이번주	this week
다음주	next week
지난달	last month
이번달	this month
다음달	next month

작년	last year
금년/ 올해	this year
내년	next year

매일	every day
일요일	Sunday
월요일	Monday
화요일	Tuesday
수요일	Wednesday
목요일	Thursday
금요일	Friday
토요일	Saturday

언제	when
생일	birthday
다음	next

Expression

몇 시예요?	What time is it?
언제 가요?	When are you going?
생일이 언제예요?	When is your birthday?
어디에 가요?	Where are you going?
생일 축하합니다.	Happy birthday.
부탁합니다.	Please (lit. asking for a favor).

II. Conversation

A: 안녕하세요!	Hello!
요즘 어떻게 지내세요?	How are you doing these days?
B: 안녕하세요!	Hello!
잘 지내요. 감사합니다.	I'm doing well. Thank you.
A: 이번 주말에 어디에 가요?	Where are you going this weekend?
B: 저는 금요일에 친구와	I'm going to the supermarket
함께 슈퍼마켓에 가요.	with my friend on Friday.
A: 몇 시에 가요?	What time are you going?
B: 오후 세 시에 가요.	I'm going at 3 PM.
그런데, 토요일에는	But on Saturday,
혼자 공원에 가요.	I'm going to the park alone.
A: 언제 돌아와요?	When will you return?
B: 저녁 여섯 시에 돌아와요.	I'll return at 6 PM.
A: 그렇군요.	I see.
다음주 월요일에 만나요!	Let's meet next Monday!
B: 네, 좋아요.	Yes, sounds good.
월요일에 학교에서 만나요.	Let's meet at school on Monday.

III. Grammar

1. Telling Time: ~시/~분 (Hour/Minute)

In Korean, 시 (hour) and 분 (minute) are used to tell the time.

- 시 is used for hours, while 분 is used for minutes.
- **Example:** 3시 30분 → "3:30"

How to use ~시/~분 (Hour/Minute)

For hours, use native Korean numbers + 시

- **Example:** 한시 (1 o'clock), 두시 (2 o'clock), 세시 (3 o'clock).

For minutes, use Sino-Korean numbers + 분.

- Example: 십 분 (10 minutes), 삼십 분 (30 minutes).

Example

i. 지금은 두시예요.

ii. 저는 여섯시에 학교에 가요.

iii. 수업은 아홉시 삼십분에 시작해요.

iv. 친구 생일 파티는 일곱시에 있어요.

v. 몇 시에 떠나요?

Telling Time in Korean

Full Hours	With Minutes
1:00 – 한시	1:15 – 한시 십오분
2:00 – 두시	2:30 – 두시 반 ("half past two")
3:00 – 세시	3:45 – 세시 사십 오분
4:00 – 네시	4:10 – 네시 십분
5:00 – 다섯시	5:20 – 다섯시 이십분
6:00 – 여섯시	6:05 – 여섯시 오분
7:00 – 일곱시	7:50 – 일곱시 오십분
8:00 – 여덟시	8:25 – 여덟시 이십 오분
9:00 – 아홉시	9:40 – 아홉시 사십분
10:00 – 열시	10:35 – 열 시삼십 오분
11:00 – 열한시	11:55 – 열한시 오십 오분
12:00 – 열두시	12:45 – 열두시 사십 오분

AM/PM

- 오전 (AM)
- 오전 9시 – 9 AM
- 오전 10시 30분 – 10:30 AM

- 오후 (PM)
- 오후 2시 – 2 PM
- 오후 3시 15분 – 3:15 PM

Note: 시 (hour): Use Native Korean numbers.

분 (minute): Use Sino-Korean numbers.

2. Days of the Week: ~요일

In Korean, each day of the week ends with 요일.

월요일 (Monday)
화요일 (Tuesday)
수요일 (Wednesday), etc.

How to Use

Simply attach 요일 to indicate a specific day.

- **Example:** "수요일에 약속이 있어요."
  (I have an appointment on Wednesday)

Example

i. 저는 금요일에 학교에 가요.
ii. 다음주 월요일에 만나요.
iii. 이번주 화요일에 회의가 있어요.
iv. 토요일에는 보통 집에 있어요.
v. 일요일에는 가족과 시간을 보내요.

3. Present Progressive Tense: ~고 있다

The present progressive tense is used to indicate actions that are happening right now.

The basic structure is verb stem + 고 있다.

- 가다 → 가고 있다 (to be going)

How to Use

Add 고 있다 to the verb stem to express ongoing actions.

- 친구가 학교에 가고 있어요.

  (The friend is going to school.)
- 저는 버스를 기다리고 있어요.

  (I am waiting for the bus.)

Example

i. 남자가 슈퍼마켓에 가고 있어요.

ii. 여자가 지하철을 타고 있어요.

iii. 친구가 학교에서 공부하고 있어요.

iv. 저는 지금 혼자 밥을 먹고 있어요.

v. 가족이 집에서 쉬고 있어요.

IV. Exercise

1. Complete the sentences with the correct time expression.

i. 지금 몇 _____예요? (What time is it now?)

ii. 저는 여덟 _____에 출발해요. (I leave at 8 o'clock.)

iii. 수업은 다섯 시 _____ 끝나요. (The class ends at 5:30.)

iv. 회의는 세 시 _____에 있어요. (The meeting is at 3:15.)

v. 점심은 열두 _____에 먹어요. (Lunch is at 12 o'clock.)

2. Match the sentences in Column A with the correct responses in Column B.

Column A
i. 몇 시예요?
ii. 다음주 월요일에 뭐 해요?
iii. 친구가 어디에 가고 있어요?
iv. 언제 슈퍼마켓에 가요?
v. 내년에는 어디에 갈 거예요?

Column B
a) 친구가 역에 가고 있어요.
b) 아침 8시예요.
c) 슈퍼마켓에 매일 가요.
d) 내년에 한국에 갈 거예요.
e) 다음주 월요일에는 회사에 가요.

3. Look at the clocks and calendars below and answer the questions in Korean.

i. 지금 몇 시예요? (Show 3:15)
ii. 다음 수요일은 언제예요? (Show next Wednesday's date)
iii. 오늘은 무슨 요일이에요? (Describe today as "Monday")
iv. 친구 생일이 5월 10일이에요. 내년 생일은 무슨 요일이에요?
v. 오늘은 금요일이에요. 내일은 무슨 요일이에요?

4. Change the following sentences into the present progressive form using ~고 있다.

i. 저는 책을 읽어요. → _____.
ii. 친구가 영화를 봐요. → _____.
iii. 엄마가 요리를 해요. → _____.
iv. 아이가 방에서 놀아요. → _____.
v. 우리는 공원에서 산책해요. → _____.

5. Complete each sentence with the correct vocabulary word from the word bank.

[기차, 가족, 일요일, 친구, 혼자]

i. 저는 _____과 여행을 가요.

ii._____에는 보통 집에서 쉬어요.

iii. 미나는 _____(서) 저녁을 먹어요.

iv. 우리는 _____를 타고 부산에 가요.

v. 내일 _____를 만날 거예요.

Chapter- 6
DESCRIBING PEOPLE

I. Vocabulary

있다	to have
없다	to not have
많다	to be many
살다	to live
같이	together
할아버지	grandfather
할머니	grandmother
아버지	father
어머니	mother
나	I
누나	older sister (if you are male or man)
형	older brother (if you are male or man)
부인	wife
언니	older sister (if you are female or woman)
오빠	older brother (if you are female or woman)
여동생	younger sister
남동생	younger brother
아들	son
딸	daughter
남자 친구	boyfriend
여자 친구	girlfriend

예쁘다	pretty
멋있다	cool
키가 크다	tall
키가 작다	short
날씬하다	skinny
뚱뚱하다	fat
재미있다	funny
친절하다	kind
똑똑하다	smart
활발하다	outgoing
얌전하다	introverted
부지런하다	diligent

Expressions

가족이 몇 명이에요?	How many family members do you have?
남자 친구/여자 친구가 있어요?	Do you have a boyfriend/girlfriend?
키가 몇이에요?	How tall are you?
누구와 같이 살아요?	Who do you live with?
정말 예쁘네요.	You are really pretty.
우리 가족은 다 친절해요.	All my family members are kind.

II. Conversation

A: 가족이 몇 명이에요?   How many family members do you have?

B: 우리 가족은 네 명이에요.   There are four people in my family:

아버지, 어머니, 형,   my father, mother, older brother,

그리고 저예요.   and me.

A: 아버지는 어떤 분이세요?   What kind of person is your father?

B: 아버지는 키가 크고,   My father is tall and

똑똑하세요.   smart.

A: 형은 어때요?   How about your older brother?

B: 형은 재미있고, 활발해요.   My older brother is funny and outgoing.

A: 어머니는요?   What about your mother?

B: 어머니는 친절하시고,   My mother is kind and

요리를 잘하세요.   good at cooking.

A: 정말 좋은 가족이네요!   You have a really nice family!

III. Grammar

1. N이/가 몇 명이에요?

This grammar pattern is used to ask about the number of people or things. In this context, it's often used to ask about the number of family members.

몇 means "how many," and it is used before the noun.

N이/가 is used to mark the subject of the sentence.

How to Use N이/가 몇 명이에요?

Attach 이/가 to the noun, then add 몇 명이에요? to ask about the number of people.

가족 + 이 → 가족이 몇 명이에요?
How many family members do you have?

Examples

i. 친구가 몇 명이에요?
ii. 가족이 몇 명이에요?
iii. 학생이 몇 명이에요?
iv. 아이들이 몇 명이에요?
v. 직원이 몇 명이에요?

2. N은/는 어떤 분이세요?

This pattern is used to ask about a person's characteristics, behavior, or personality.

어떤 means "what kind of" or "how," and 분 is an honorific term for "person."

은/는 is used to emphasize the subject.

How to Use N은/는 어떤 분이세요?

Attach 은/는 to the noun, followed by 어떤 분이세요? to ask about someone's characteristics.

아버지 + 는 → 아버지는 어떤 분이세요?
(What kind of person is your father?)

Examples

i. 할아버지는 어떤 분이세요?
ii. 친구는 어떤 사람인가요?
iii. 선생님은 어떤 분이세요?
iv. 남자 친구는 어떤 분이세요?
v. 할머니는 어떤 분이세요?

3. N은/는 Adjective + 고, Adjective + 해요

This pattern is used to describe someone or something with multiple adjectives in one sentence.

The conjunction 고 is used to connect two or more adjectives, similar to "and" in English.

은/는 emphasizes the noun being described.

How to Use N은/는 Adjective + 고, Adjective + 하세요.

Attach 은/는 to the noun, then add the first adjective + 고, followed by the second adjective + 하세요.

형은 재미있고, 활발하세요.
My older brother is funny and outgoing.

Examples

i. 어머니는 예쁘시고 친절하세요
ii. 친구는 똑똑하고 부지런하세요
iii. 아버지는 키가 크고 멋있으세요.
iv. 할머니는 조용하고 부지런하세요.
v. 여동생은 날씬하고 활발하세요.

IV. Exercise

1. Fill in the Blanks

i. _____이 몇 명이에요? (family)

ii. _____가 몇 명이에요? (friend)

iii. _____이 몇 명 있어요? (younger siblings)

iv. 회사에 _____이 몇 명이에요? (employees)

v. 학교에 _____이 몇 명이에요? (students)

2. Use the adjectives to complete the sentences.

i. 어머니는 예쁘다 / 친절하다

　어머니는 _____시고 _____하세요.

ii. 형은 키가 크다 / 멋있다

　형은 _____고 _____요.

iii. 할머니는 부지런하다 / 조용하다

　　할머니는 _____고 _____하세요.

iv. 여동생은 날씬하다 / 활발하다

　　여동생은 _____고 _____하세요.

v. 아버지는 키가 크다 / 똑똑하다

　아버지는 _____고 _____세요.

3. Complete the Sentences using correct grammar form.

Example: 할아버지: 부지런하다 / 친절하다

할아버지는 부지런하시고 친절하세요.

i. 형: 키가 크다 / 멋있다

_____

ii. 어머니: 예쁘다 / 요리를 잘하다

_____

iii. 여동생: 날씬하다 / 활발하다

_____

iv. 아버지: 키가 크다/ 똑똑하다

_____

4. Translate the following sentences using the grammar patterns.

i. How many siblings do you have?

ii. My grandmother is kind and diligent.

iii. I have two younger sisters.

iv. My father is tall and smart.

v. What kind of person is your brother?

Note: Translations may vary based on vocabulary and phrasing. We have included potential translations in answer keys for each but keep in mind that other translations would work as well.

5. Read the passage and answer the following questions

지수의 가족은 다섯 명이에요. 아버지, 어머니, 할머니, 여동생, 그리고 지수예요. 아버지는 키가 크고 부지런하세요. 어머니는 예쁘시고 요리를 잘하세요. 할머니는 친절하고 얌전하세요. 여동생은 날씬하고 활발해요. 지수는 똑똑하고 재미있어요. 지수의 가족은 모두 서울에 같이 살아요.

i. 지수의 가족은 몇 명이에요?
a) 네 명
b) 다섯 명
c) 여섯 명

ii. 아버지는 어떤 분이세요?
a) 키가 작고 얌전하세요.
b) 키가 크고 부지런하세요.
c) 예쁘시고 요리를 잘하세요.

iii. 할머니는 어떤 분이세요?
a) 친절하시고 얌전하세요.
b) 재미있으시고 활발해요.
c) 똑똑하시고 날씬하세요.

iv. 지수의 여동생은 어떤 사람이에요?
a) 키가 크고 부지런해요.
b) 날씬하고 활발해요.
c) 예쁘고 요리를 잘해요.

v. 지수의 가족은 어디에 살아요?
a) 부산
b) 인천
c) 서울

Chapter- 7

I. Vocabulary

먹다	to eat
마시다	to drink
사다	to buy
가다	to go
오다	to come
보다	to see/watch
읽다	to read
쓰다	to write
만들다	to make
열다	to open
닫다	to close
도와주다	to help
기다리다	to wait
앉다	to sit
일어나다	to stand up
청소하다	to clean
전화하다	to call
주다	to give
듣다	to listen
배우다	to learn
준비하다	to prepare
요리하다	to cook

음식	food
물	water
책	book
창문	window
문	door
선물	gift
전화	phone
편지	letter
방	room
차	tea/car
밥	rice/meal
커피	coffee
공	ball
옷	clothes
신발	shoes
가방	bag

Expressions

잠깐만 기다려 주세요.	Please wait a moment.
도와주세요.	Please help me.
다시 말해 주세요.	Please say it again.
이거 사 주세요.	Please buy this for me.
창문을 열어 주세요.	Please open the window.
물 좀 주세요.	Please give me some water.
잠시만요.	Just a moment.

II. Conversation

A: 어서 오세요!	Welcome!
무엇을 도와드릴까요?	How can I help you?
B: 물 좀 주세요.	Please give me some water.
A: 네, 잠시만요.	Sure, just a moment.
B: 이 책도 읽어 주세요.	Please read this book, too.
A: 알겠습니다.	Got it.
그리고 문을 닫아 주시겠어요?	And could you close the door, please?
B: 네, 그렇게 할게요.	Yes, I will do that.
A: 감사합니다!	Thank you!
B: 천만에요.	You're welcome.

III. Grammar

1. Polite Requests: ~(으)세요

This form is used to make polite requests or commands.

~으세요 is used after verbs ending with a consonant.

~세요 is used after verbs ending with a vowel.

How to Use ~(으)세요

Verb stem + (으)세요.

Eg: 먹다 → 먹으세요 (Please eat).

가다 → 가세요 (Please go).

Examples

i. 이거 보세요.

ii. 책을 읽으세요.

iii. 밥을 드세요.

iv. 창문을 여세요.

v. 여기 앉으세요.

2. Imperative Form: ~아/어 주세요

This form is used to ask someone to do something for you, indicating a more personal or direct request.

~아 주세요 is used if the verb stem ends in ㅏ or ㅗ.

~어 주세요 is used for all other verb endings.

How to Use ~아/어 주세요

Verb stem + 아/어 주세요.

Eg: 사다 → 사 주세요 (Please buy this for me).

열다 → 열어 주세요 (Please open it for me).

Examples

i. 물 좀 주세요.

ii. 이 책을 읽어 주세요.

iii. 도와주세요.

iv. 이거 만들어 주세요.

v. 문을 닫아 주세요.

3. Honorific Requests: ~시겠어요?

This is a polite and formal way to make requests, used to show respect or deference to the person being addressed.

The verb stem is followed by 시겠어요 to ask someone to do something in a respectful manner.

How to Use ~시겠어요?

Verb stem + 시겠어요?

Eg: 도와주다 → 도와주시겠어요? (Could you help me?)

앉다 → 앉으시겠어요? (Would you please sit down?)

Examples

i. 이거 좀 열어주시겠어요?

ii. 저를 도와주시겠어요?

iii. 차를 준비해 주시겠어요?

iv. 방을 청소해 주시겠어요?

v. 잠시 기다려 주시겠어요?

IV. Exercise

1. Complete the sentences with the correct form of ~(으)세요.

i. 이 책을 _____ (읽다).

ii. 물을 _____ (마시다).

iii. 방을 _____ (청소하다).

iv. 여기 _____ (오다).

v. 이거 _____ (보내다).

2. Match the requests in Column A with the correct actions in Column B.

Column A	Column B
i. 물 좀 _____	a) 도와
ii. 문을 _____ 주세요.	b) 준비해
iii. 저를 _____ 주세요.	c) 닫아
iv. 차를 _____ 주세요.	d) 써
v. 편지를 _____ 주세요.	e) 주세요

3. Make polite requests (~시겠어요?)

i. 전화하다 → 전화해 주시겠어요?

ii. 기다리다 → _____ 주시겠어요?

iii. 앉다 → _____ 주시겠어요?

iv. 도와주다 → _____ 주시겠어요?

v. 열다 → _____ 주시겠어요?

4. Translate the following sentences into Korean.

i. Please open the door.

ii. Could you help me, please?

iii. Would you please wait a moment?

iv. Please write this letter for me.

v. Please give me some coffee.

5. Rearrange the words to form correct sentences using the polite request patterns.

i. 주세요 / 물 / 좀 /

ii. 도와 / 주시겠어요 / 저를 / ?

iii. 창문 / 열어 / 주세요 / 을

iv. 앉으세요 / 여기 /

v. 기다려 / 주세요 / 잠깐만

Chapter- 8
ASKING QUESTIONS

I. Vocabulary

말하다	to speak/ say or talk
배우다	to learn
일하다	to work
기다리다	to wait
쉬다	to rest
시작하다	to start
끝나다	to finish
주다	to give
타다	to ride
선택하다	to choose/ to select
찾다	to find
결정하다	to decide
보내다	to send
받다	to receive
잃어버리다	to lose
도착하다	to arrive
떠나다	to leave
생각하다	to think
수업	class
시간	time
장소	place

일	work
공항	airport
길	road
기분	mood
음식점	restaurant
영화관	movie theater
병원	hospital/ Clinic
주말	weekend
계획	plan
문제	problem
방법	method
약속	promise/ appointments
물건	object/ thing
길	road/ way
뭐/ 무엇	what
어디	where
언제	when
누구	who
왜	why
어떻게	how
어떤	what kind of

Expressions

뭐 해요?   What are you doing?

어디 가요?   Where are you going?

언제 만나요?   When are we meeting?

누구를 기다려요?   Who are you waiting for?

어떤 음식을 좋아해요?   What kind of food do you like?

어떻게 가요?   How do you go?

왜 그래요?   Why is that?

II. Conversation

A: 어디에 가요?   A: Where are you going?

B: 저는 병원에 가요.   B: I am going to the hospital.

A: 왜 병원에 가요?   A: Why are you going to the hospital?

B: 몸이 아파서 병원에 가요. B: I am going because I feel sick.

A: 언제 도착할까요?   A: When will we arrive?

B: 30분 후에 도착할 거예요. B: We will arrive in 30 minutes.

A: 어떤 음식을 먹을까요?   A: What kind of food shall we eat?

B: 한국 음식을 먹을까요?   B: Shall we eat Korean food?

A: 네, 좋아요!   A: Yes, sounds good!

III. Grammar

1. Wh- Questions: 무엇/뭐, 어디, 언제, 누구

These words are used to form open-ended questions in Korean.

- 무엇/뭐 (What): Used to ask about things or activities.
- 어디 (Where): Used to ask about places or locations.
- 언제 (When): Used to ask about time.
- 누구/ 누가 (Who): Used to ask about people.

How to Use 무엇/뭐, 어디, 언제, 누구

Place the Wh- question word at the beginning or within the sentence.

Eg: 뭐 해요? (What are you doing?)

어디에 가요? (Where are you going?)

언제 와요? (When are you coming?)

누구와 같이 가요? (Who are you going with?)

Examples

i. 지금 뭐 해요?

ii. 어디에서 일해요?

iii. 내일 언제 만나요?

iv. 누구를 기다려요?

2. "What kind" Questions: 어떤 (What kind of)

어떤 is used to ask about the type or kind of something. It is usually placed before the noun it describes.

How to Use

어떤 + **Noun** + **Verb?**

Eg: 어떤 영화가 좋아요? (What kind of movie do you like?)

어떤 음식이 맛있어요? (What kind of food is delicious?)

Examples

i. 어떤 음악을 들어요?

ii. 어떤 음식을 좋아해요?

iii. 어떤 일을 하고 싶어요?

iv. 어떤 색을 좋아해요?

3. Forming Questions: Verb + 까요?

This pattern is used to form questions in a casual yet polite way. It's often used to make suggestions, ask for confirmation, or check someone's intention.

Attach 까요? directly to the verb stem.

How to Use

Verb stem + 까요?

Eg: 같이 갈까요? (Shall we go together?)

뭐 먹을까요? (What should we eat?)

Examples

i. 언제 만날까요?

ii. 무엇을 볼까요?

iii. 어디에서 먹을까요?

iv. 커피 마실까요?

v. 지금 떠날까요?

IV. Exercise

1. Fill in the Blank (Wh- Questions)

i. _____ 해요?

ii. _____ 가요?

iii. 내일 _____ 만나요?

iv. _____를 기다려요?

v. _____ 음식을 좋아해요?

vi. 시험은 _____ 시작해요?

2. Match the questions in Column A with the correct responses in Column B.

Column A	Column B
i. 어떤 음악을 좋아해요?	a) 저는 액션 영화를 보고 싶어요.
ii. 어떤 영화를 보고 싶어요?	b) 저는 클래식 음악을 좋아해요.
iii. 어떤 음식을 먹을까요?	c) 저는 한국 음식을 먹고 싶어요.
iv. 어떤 일을 하고 싶어요?	d) 저는 선생님이 되고 싶어요.

3. Form questions using the given words and grammar patterns.

    Eg: (뭐, 하다, 지금) → 지금 뭐 해요?

  i. (뭐, 먹다, 지금) → _____?

  ii. (누구, 전화하다, 지금) → _____?

  iii. (어디, 일하다, 친구) → _____?

  iv. (언제, 도착하다, 버스) → _____?

  v. (왜, 늦다, 오늘) → _____?

4. Form sentences using the Verb + 까요? pattern to suggest an action or ask for opinions.

    Eg: (커피, 마시다) → 커피를 마실까요?

  i. (영화, 보다) → _____?

  ii. (밥, 먹다, 지금) → _____?

  iii. (산책, 가다, 주말) → _____?

  iv. (어디, 가다, 내일) → _____?

  v. (커피, 마시다, 같이) → _____?

5. Fill in the blanks using correct vocabulary from word bank.

> 말하다, 주다, 일하다, 배우다, 받다, 끝나다, 타다, 보내다

  i. 저는 한국어를 _____ 있어요.

  ii. 오늘 수업은 3시에 _____.

  iii. 그는 친구에게 선물을 _____.

  iv. 버스를 _____ 가요.

  v. 편지를 _____ 주세요.

Chapter- 9

I. Vocabulary

영화	movie/ film
여행	trip/travel
음악	music
춤	dance
그림	painting/drawing
운동	exercise/sports
축구	soccer/ football
책	book
편지	letter
연극	play/drama
음식	food
빵	bread
커피	coffee
차	tea
산책	walk
사진	photo/picture
동물	animal
날씨	weather
집	house
꽃	flower
바다	sea

산	mountain
강	river
학교	school
시장	market
공원	park
음식점	restaurant
도서관	library
기차	train
버스	bus
텔레비전	television
뉴스	news
아침/아침 식사	breakfast
저녁/저녁 식사	dinner
점심/점심 식사	lunch
먹다	to eat/to have a meal
마시다	to drink
가다	to go
보다	to see/watch
읽다	to read
듣다	to listen
만나다	to meet

배우다	to learn
찍다	to take (a photo)
쉬다	to rest
걷다	to walk

Expressions

저는 빵을 먹고 싶어요.	I want to eat bread.
이 영화를 보고 싶어요.	I want to watch this movie.
저는 커피를 좋아해요.	I like coffee.
그녀는 춤을 싫어해요.	She dislikes dancing.
무엇을 먹고 싶어요?	What do you want to eat?
어디에 가고 싶어요?	Where do you want to go?

II. Conversation

A: 뭐 하고 싶어요?	What do you want to do?
B: 저는 영화를 보고 싶어요.	I want to watch a movie.
A: 어떤 영화를	What kind of movie
보고 싶어요?	do you want to watch?
B: 코미디 영화를 보고 싶어요.	I want to watch a comedy movie.
A: 저는 코미디 영화를	I dislike comedy
싫어해요.	movies.
B: 그럼, 음악을 들을까요?	Then, shall we listen to music?
A: 네, 저는 음악을 좋아해요.	Yes, I like music.

III. Grammar

1. Verb + ~고 싶다 (To want to...)

This pattern is used to express a desire to do something. It is formed by attaching ~고 싶다 to the verb stem.

How to Use

Verb stem + ~고 싶다.

Eg: • 가다 → 가고 싶다 (to want to go).

• 보다 → 보고 싶다 (to want to see/watch).

Examples

i.   저는 영화를 보고 싶어요.

ii.   커피를 마시고 싶어요.

iii. 오늘은 쉬고 싶어요.

iv.   산책하고 싶어요.

v.   저녁을 먹고 싶어요.

2. Verb + ~을/를 좋아하다 (To like)

This pattern is used to express liking something. 좋아하다 is used after the object particle 을/를, depending on whether the noun ends in a consonant or a vowel.

How to Use

Noun + 을/를 좋아하다.

Eg: • 책 → 책을 좋아하다 (to like books).

• 영화 → 영화를 좋아하다 (to like movies).

Examples

i. 저는 축구를 좋아해요.

ii. 그녀는 음악을 좋아해요.

iii. 친구는 커피를 좋아해요.

iv. 저는 동물을 좋아해요.

v. 우리는 빵을 좋아해요.

3. Verb + ~을/를 싫어하다 (To dislike)

This pattern is used to express disliking something. 싫어하다 is used similarly to 좋아하다, following the object particle 을/를.

How to Use

Noun + 을/를 싫어하다.

Eg: • 책 → 책을 싫어하다 (to dislike books).

• 영화 → 영화를 싫어하다 (to dislike movies).

Examples

i. 저는 춤을 싫어해요.

ii. 그녀는 운동을 싫어해요.

iii. 그는 야채를 싫어해요.

iv. 아이는 병원을 싫어해요.

v. 저는 기차를 싫어해요.

IV. Exercise

1. Complete the sentences using the ~고 싶다 form.

i. 저는 커피를 _____ 싶어요.

ii. 오늘 산책을 _____ 싶어요.

iii. 친구를 _____ 싶어요.

iv. 편지를 _____ 싶어요.

v. 빵을 _____ 싶어요.

2. Match the sentences in Column A with the appropriate responses in Column B.

Column A	Column B
i. 저는 커피를 좋아해요.	a) He likes animals.
ii. 그녀는 책을 좋아해요.	b) I like coffee.
iii. 그는 동물을 좋아해요.	c) She likes books.
iv. 우리는 축구를 좋아해요.	d) The child likes bread.
v. 아이는 빵을 좋아해요.	e) We like soccer.

3. Fill in the Blanks (Mix of Patterns)

i. 저는 차를 _____ 싶어요. (I want to drink tea.)

ii. 그녀는 영화를 _____. (She likes movies.)

iii. 그는 빵을 _____. (He dislikes bread.)

iv. 우리는 음악을 _____. (We like music.)

v. 아이들은 시장에 _____ 싶어요. (Kids want to go to the market.).

4. Translate the following English sentences into Korean using the correct grammar patterns.

    i. I want to go to the park.

    ii. She likes to drink tea.

    iii. He dislikes exercising.

    iv. Do you want to watch television?

    v. I like reading books.

5. Answer "Yes" (네) or "No" (아니요) based on your preferences.

    i. 축구를 좋아해요?

    ii. 커피를 싫어해요?

    iii.   산에 가고 싶어요?

    iv.   책을 읽고 싶어요?

    v. 동물을 좋아해요?

    vi.   시장에 가고 싶어요?

    vii.   바다를 싫어해요?

Chapter- 10
ABILITIES AND INTENTIONS

I. Vocabulary

운전	driving
수영	swimming
요가	yoga
요리	cooking
청소	cleaning
달리기	running
등산	hiking
자전거 타기	cycling
악기 연주	playing an instrument
노래	singing
춤추기	dancing
쇼핑	shopping
낚시	fishing
야구	baseball
농구	basketball
테니스	tennis
배드민턴	badminton
조깅	jogging
축구	football/soccer
여행	traveling/trip

캠핑	camping
말하기	speaking
듣기	listening
쓰레기 버리기	taking out the trash
설거지	washing the dishes
빨래하기	doing the laundry
그림 그리기	drawing/painting
사진 찍기	taking photos
책 읽기	reading a book
영화 보기	watching a movie
방문	visiting
산책	taking a walk

Expressions

할 수 있어요	Can do
할 수 없어요	Cannot do
하려고 해요	Plan/Intend to do
하는 것	Doing (noun form of verbs)
좋아해요	Like (used after nouns)
싫어해요	Dislike (used after nouns)
잘 할 수 있어요	Can do well
배우려고 해요	Plan to learn

II. Conversation

A: 무슨 운동을 할 수 있어요? What sports can you do?

B: 저는 축구를 할 수 있어요. I can play football.

A: 요리할 수 있어요? Can you cook?

B: 아니요, 요리를 잘 할 수 없어요. No, I can't cook well.

그런데 배우려고 해요. But I plan to learn.

A: 자전거 타는 것은 어때요? How about cycling?

B: 자전거 타는 것을 좋아해요! I like cycling!

III. Grammar

1. Verb + (으)ㄹ 수 있다/없다: Can/Can't do

This pattern is used to express the ability or inability to do something.

- (으)ㄹ 수 있다: Can do.

- ~(으)ㄹ 수 없다: Can't do.

- Use (으)ㄹ after verb stems ending with a consonant (except for ㄹ), and ㄹ after vowel-ending verb stems or verb stems ending in ㄹ.

How to Use

Verb stem + (으)ㄹ 수 있다/없다.

Eg:
- 수영하다 → 수영할 수 있다 (can swim).
- 요리하다 → 요리할 수 없다 (can't cook).

Examples

i. 저는 수영할 수 있어요.

ii. 요리를 잘 할 수 있어요.

iii. 운전을 할 수 없어요.

iv. 저는 달리기를 할 수 없어요.

v. 악기를 연주할 수 있어요.

2. Verb + (으)ㄴ/는 것: Turning Verbs into Nouns

This pattern turns verbs into nouns, enabling you to use actions as subjects or objects in a sentence.

- Verb stem + (으)ㄴ/는 것 means "doing something" or "the act of doing."
- Use (으)ㄴ 것 for past actions and 는 것 for present actions.

How to Use

Verb stem + (으)ㄴ/는 것.

Eg: • 요리하다 → 요리하는 것 (cooking).

• 운전하다 → 운전하는 것 (driving).

Examples

i. 요리하는 것은 재미있어요.

ii. 수영하는 것을 좋아해요.

iii. 산책하는 것은 건강에 좋아요.

iv. 그림 그리는 것은 어려워요.

v. 자전거 타는 것을 즐겨요.

3. Verb + (으)려고 하다: Expressing Intention to Do Something

This pattern is used to express one's intention or plan to do something.

- Use (으)려고 하다 after the verb stem.

- Use 으려고 if the verb stem ends in a consonant,

and 려고 if it ends in a vowel.

How to Use

Verb stem + (으)려고 하다

Eg: • 운전하다 → 운전하려고 하다 (to intend to drive).

• 수영하다 → 수영하려고 하다 (to intend to swim).

Examples

i. 저는 수영을 배우려고 해요.

ii. 요리를 하려고 해요.

iii. 오늘 쇼핑하려고 해요.

iv. 악기를 연주하려고 해요.

v. 산책을 하려고 해요.

IV. Exercise

1. Using the prompts, create sentences that express your abilities, intentions, or opinions.

Eg: 할 수 있어요: 저는 수영할 수 있어요.

i. 하려고 해요

ii. 좋아해요

iii. 중요해요

iv. 재미없어요

2. Match the Korean phrases in Column A with their corresponding meanings in Column B.

Column A	Column B
i. 할 수 있어요	a) Plan to learn
ii. 배우려고 해요	b) Difficult
iii. 어려워요	c) Can do
iv. 좋아해요	d) Not fun
v. 재미없어요	e) Important
vi. 할 수 없어요	f) Good for health
vii. 건강에 좋아요	g) Cannot do
viii. 중요해요	h) Like
ix. 즐겨요	i) Not easy
x. 쉽지 않아요	j) Enjoy

3. Turn the following verbs into nouns using (으)ㄴ/는 것.

Eg: 좋아하다 → 좋아하는 것

i. 청소하다 → _____

ii. 조깅하다 → _____

iii. 책 읽다 → _____

iv. 그림 그리다 → _____

v. 달리기 → _____

4. Read the paragraph and complete it by filling in the blanks with the appropriate expressions from the list.

> 할 수 있어요, 좋아해요, 하려고 해요,
> 중요해요, 즐겨요, 중요해요

저는 운동하는 것 아주 i.) _____. 그래서 매일 아침에 조깅을 합니다. 조깅은 건강에 ii.) _____ 그리고 재미있이요. 주말에는 친구들과 축구를 합니다. 축구하는 것은 조금 힘들지만, 저는 정말 iii.) _____. 요즘 저는 수영을 배우려고 합니다. 수영은 처음에 어렵지만 연습하면 잘 iv.) _____. 또한, 요리하는 것을 배우고 싶어요. 요리는 건강을 위해서 아주 v.) _____. 앞으로 더 많은 요리를 vi.) _____.

5. Translate the following sentences into Korean using the correct grammar pattern

i. I enjoy cycling.

ii. Cooking is important.

iii. Playing soccer is fun.

iv. I plan to learn swimming.

v. Yoga is not easy.

Chapter- 11
TALKING ABOUT THE PAST

I. Vocabulary

여행	trip/travel
졸업	graduation
결혼식	wedding
생일 파티	birthday party
기념일	anniversary
휴가	vacation
방학	school break
소풍	picnic
운동회	sports event
축제	festival
회의	meeting
콘서트	concert
전시회	exhibition
영화 관람	movie viewing
음식 축제	food festival
문화 체험	cultural experience
봉사 활동	volunteer activity
취업	getting a job
입학	entering school
이사	moving house
방문	visit

입원	hospitalization
퇴원	discharge from hospital
독서	reading
공연	performance
대화	conversation
토론	debate
사진 전시회	photo exhibition
대회	competition
발표	presentation
일기	diary
소식/뉴스	news
편지 작성	writing a letter

Expressions

가 본 적 있어요	Have been to
해 본 적 있어요	Have tried
먹어 본 적 있어요	Have eaten
봤어요	Saw/Watched
만났어요	Met
갔어요	Went
했어요	Did
소식	Heard

II. Conversation

A: 주말에 뭐 했어요?

B: 저는 친구와 함께
소풍을 갔어요.

A: 어디로 갔어요?

B: 서울 공원에 갔어요.
김밥을 먹어 본 적 있어요?

A: 네, 먹어 본 적 있어요.
정말 맛있었어요!

B: 저도 그렇게 생각해요.

What did you do over the weekend?

I went on a picnic
with a friend.

Where did you go?

I went to Seoul Park.

Have you tried kimbap?

Yes, I have tried it.

It was really delicious!

I think so, too.

III. Grammar

1. Past Tense: ~았/었

This pattern is used to express past actions or events.

- ~았 is used for verb stems ending in ㅏ or ㅗ.
- ~었 is used for other verb endings.

How to Use

Verb stem + 았/었.

Eg: • 가다 → 갔어요 (went),
• 먹다 → 먹었어요 (ate).

Examples

i. 저는 어제 영화를 봤어요.

ii. 친구를 만났어요.

iii. 서울에 갔어요.

iv. 점심을 먹었어요.

v. 책을 읽었어요.

2. Expressing Past Actions: ~했어요

This pattern is used to describe past actions that have been completed, often used with 하다 verbs.

How to Use

Verb stem + 했어요

Eg: • 공부하다 → 공부했어요 (studied),

• 운동하다 → 운동했어요 (exercised)

Examples

i. 저는 어제 운동했어요.

ii. 친구와 이야기했어요.

iii. 한국 음식을 요리했어요.

iv. 지난 주에 여행했어요.

v. 주말에 청소했어요.

3. Narrating Experiences: ~본 적 있다 (Have done something)

This pattern is used to narrate experiences that have happened at least once in the past.

Attach 본 적 있다 after the verb stem to express having done something before.

How to Use

Verb stem + 본 적 있다

Eg: • 먹다 → 먹어 본 적 있다 (have eaten),

• 가다 → 가 본 적 있다 (have been)

Examples

i. 일본에 가 본 적 있어요.

ii. 김치를 먹어 본 적 있어요.

iii. 그 영화를 본 적 있어요.

iv. 피아노를 쳐 본 적 있어요.

v. 자전거를 타 본 적 있어요.

4. Using 'Before': ~전에

~전에 is used to indicate that an action or event occurred before another action or specific point in time. It emphasizes the temporal sequence, showing what preceded the referenced action or moment.

How to Use

Verb stem + 기 전에 (before doing something)

Eg: • 먹다 → 먹기 전에 (before eating),

• 가다 → 가기 전에 (before going).

Examples

i. 학교에 가기 전에 아침을 먹었어요.

ii. 영화를 보기 전에 예매했어요.

iii. 운동하기 전에 물을 마셨어요.

iv. 일을 시작하기 전에 계획을 세웠어요.

v. 친구를 만나기 전에 선물을 샀어요.

IV. Exercise

1. Convert the following verbs into the correct past tense form based on the context.

i. 어제 친구를 (만나다) → _____.

ii. 주말에 가족과 (산책하다) → _____.

iii. 지난달에 새로운 집으로 (이사하다) → _____.

iv. 지난밤에 영화를 (보다) → _____.

v. 아침에 신문을 (읽다) → _____.

2. Convert the following verbs into ~본 적 있다 to describe experiences.

i. 여행하다 → _____

ii. 김치를 먹다 → _____

iii. 일본에 가다 → _____

iv. 피아노를 치다 → _____

v. 자전거를 타다 → _____

3. Rearrange the words to form correct past tense sentences.

i. 갔어요 / 저는 / 서울에 / 어제

ii. 봤어요 / 영화를 / 지난밤에 / 친구와

iii. 만났어요 / 주말에 / 친구를 / 저는

iv. 어제 / 요리했어요 / 저녁을 / 저는

v. 읽었어요 / 책을 / 저는 / 아침에

4. Match the sentence fragments in Column A with the correct endings in Column B.

Column A	Column B
i. 저는 지난주에 제주도에	a) 영화를 봤어요.
ii. 어제 친구와 카페에서	b) 이사를 했어요.
iii. 작년에 새 아파트로	c) 여행을 갔어요.
iv. 지난밤에 집에서	d) 운동했어요.
v. 아침에 공원에서	e) 만났어요.

5. Read the following paragraph and fill in the blanks with the appropriate past tense forms, expressions, or phrases from the Word Bank.

> 갔어요, 봤어요, 읽었어요, 먹어 본 적 있어요,
> 여행했어요, 전시회에서, 전에

지난주에 저는 친구와 함께 서울로 i.) _____. 우리는 서울에서 서울에 있는 유명한 미술 ii.) _____ 많은 그림을 보았습니다. 저는 그중에서 추상화를 특히 좋아했어요. 그 후에 우리는 근처의 한국 음식점에 갔어요. 거기서 김치를 iii.) _____. 저는 김치를 여러 번 iv.) _____ 그래서 매운 맛에 익숙해요. 저녁에는 호텔로 돌아와서 책을 v.) _____. 그리고 자기 vi.) _____ 친구와 함께 그날의 일에 대해 이야기했어요.

Chapter- 12

FUTURE PLANS AND POSSIBILITIES

I. Vocabulary

계획	plan
미래	future
다음 주	next week
다음 달	next month
내년	next year
약속	appointment/promise
여행	trip/travel
결혼	wedding
생일 파티	birthday party
행사	event
면접	interview
대학 입학	university admission
시험	exam
시작	start
준비	preparation
이사	moving house
졸업식	graduation ceremony
기대	expectation
공연	performance
방문	visit
축제	festival

쇼핑	shopping
데이트	date
공부	studying
운동	exercise
취업	employment
진학	advancement to school
전시회	exhibition
콘서트	concert
작업	work
산책	walk

Expressions

배울 거예요	Will learn
들릴 것 같아요	Will probably hear
올 것 같아요	Will probably come
시작하려고 해요	Plan to start
이사하려고 해요	Plan to move
기다릴 것 같아요	Will probably wait
준비하려고 해요	Plan to prepare
취업할 거예요	Will get a job
기대하고 있어요	Looking forward to it
만날 거예요	Will meet
생각 중이에요	Thinking about it

II. Conversation

A: 주말에 뭐 할 거예요?
B: 저는 가족과 함께
여행 갈 거예요.
A: 어디로 갈 거예요?
B: 아마 제주도에 갈 것 같아요.
A: 저는 집에서 쉬려고 해요.
B: 그럼, 나중에 같이
만나서 저녁 먹을까요?
A: 네, 좋아요.

What will you do over the weekend?
I will go on a trip
with my family.
Where will you go?
Maybe we will go to Jeju Island.
I plan to rest at home.
Then, shall we meet l
ater for dinner?
Yes, sounds good.

III. Grammar

1. Future Tense: ~ㄹ/을 거예요

Used to express actions that will happen in the future.

- Attach ~ㄹ 거예요 to verb stems ending with a vowel.
- Attach ~을 거예요 to verb stems ending with a consonant.

How to Use

Verb stem + ~ㄹ/을 거예요.

Eg: • 가다 → 갈 거예요 (will go),

• 먹다 → 먹을 거예요 (will eat).

Examples

i. 저는 내일 서울에 갈 거예요.
ii. 우리는 저녁에 영화를 볼 거예요.
iii. 그는 다음 달에 졸업할 거예요.
iv. 친구를 만날 거예요.
v. 한국어를 배울 거예요.

2. Plans and Intentions: ~려고 하다

Used to express plans or intentions to do something.

- Attach ~려고 하다 after the verb stem to indicate intention.

How to Use

Verb stem + ~려고 하다.

Eg: • 요리하다 → 요리하려고 하다 (plan to cook),

- 여행하다 → 여행하려고 하다 (plan to travel).

Examples

i. 저는 다음 주에 이사하려고 해요.
ii. 친구와 같이 여행하려고 해요.
iii. 한국어를 더 열심히 배우려고 해요
iv. 새로운 직업을 찾으려고 해요.
v. 내년에 대학에 가려고 해요.

3. Expressing Probability: ~ㄹ/을 것 같다

Used to express the probability or likelihood of something happening.

- Attach ~ㄹ 것 같다 to verb stems ending with a vowel.
- Attach ~을 것 같다 to verb stems ending with a consonant.

How to Use

Verb stem + ~ㄹ/을 것 같다.

Eg: • 가다 → 갈 것 같다 (will probably go),

- 오다 → 올 것 같다 (will probably come).

Examples

i. 내일 비가 올 것 같아요.

ii. 그는 시험에 합격할 것 같아요.

iii. 이번 주말에 바빠질 것 같아요.

iv. 새로운 영화를 볼 것 같아요.

v. 그녀가 파티에 올 것 같아요.

4. Using "Maybe": 아마 ~르/을 거예요

아마 is used to express uncertainty or possibility about future events.

- Combine it with the future tense form ~르/을 거예요.

How to Use

아마 + **Verb stem** + ~르/을 거예요.

Eg: • 가다 → 아마 갈 거예요 (maybe will go).

Examples

i. 아마 내일 비가 올 거예요.

ii. 아마 그가 이길 거예요.

iii. 아마 우리는 늦을 거예요.

iv. 아마 새 차를 살 거예요.

v. 아마 주말에 만날 거예요.

IV. Exercise

1. Complete each sentence using the ~르/을 거예요 form.

i. 저는 내년에 대학에 _____. (enter)

ii. 친구와 같이 영화를 _____. (watch)

iii. 우리는 내일 서울로 _____. (go)

iv. 주말에 새로운 책을 _____. (read)

v. 그는 다음 달에 이사를 _____. (move)

2. Convert the following verbs to express plans or intentions using ~려고 하다.

i. 공부하다 → _____

ii. 요리하다 → _____

iii. 이사하다 → _____

iv. 여행하다 → _____

v. 만나다 → _____

3. Complete the Sentences (Using ~르 것 같다)

Eg: 오늘 날씨가 <u>맑을 것 같아요.</u>

i. 우리는 내일 일찍 _____. (leave)

ii. 그녀가 시험에 _____. (pass)

iii. 이번 주말에 비가 _____. (rain)

iv. 저녁에 친구를 _____. (meet)

4. Using the prompts, create sentences that describe future plans or probabilities.

Eg: (내년, 가다, 여행) → <u>내년에 여행을 갈 거예요.</u>

i. (아침, 하다, 운동) → _____

ii. (이번 주말, 만나다, 친구) → _____

iii. (오늘 저녁. 먹다, 비빔밥) → _____

iv. (다음 주, 준비하다, 시험) → _____

v. (주말, 보다, 영화) → _____

5. Translate the following sentences into Korean using the correct grammar patterns.

i. I will start studying next month.

ii. We will probably go to the festival this weekend.

iii. I plan to move to Seoul next year.

iv. Maybe I will visit my friend tomorrow.

v. She will probably graduate in June.

Chapter- 13

I. Vocabulary

키	height
무게	weight
가격	price
속도	speed
온도	temperature
길이	length
맛	taste
크기	size
외모	appearance
성격	personality
경험	experience
지식	knowledge
성능	performance
건강	health
효율	efficiency
운동	exercise
장점	advantage
단점	disadvantage
기분	mood
기억	memory

지혜	wisdom
미래	future
성공	success
실패	failure
기회	opportunity
사람	person
직업	job
음식	food
옷	clothes
집	house
차	car
여행	trip
날씨	weather

Expressions

가장 비싸요	most expensive
이것보다 더 좋아요	better than this
저것보다 더 나빠요	worse than that
더 맛있어요	tastier
더 예뻐요	prettier
더 건강해요	healthier
이 사람보다 더 똑똑해요	smarter than this person
이 차가 가장 빨라요	this car is the fastest
이 음식이 가장 맛있어요	this food is the most delicious

II. Conversation

A: 어떤 차가 더 빨라요?　　　　Which car is faster?

B: 이 차가 저 차보다 더 빨라요.　This car is faster than that car.

A: 그렇군요. 그럼,　　　　　　　I see. Then, which is

가장 비싼 차는 뭐예요?　　　　the most expensive car?

B: 이 차가 가장 비싸요.　　　　This car is the most expensive.

A: 나는 자전거보다　　　　　　I like cars more

차를 더 좋아해요.　　　　　　than bicycles.

B: 나도 그래요.　　　　　　　Me too.

III. Grammar

1. Comparatives: ~보다 더 (Than)

~보다 더 is used to make comparisons, indicating that one thing is more than another.

- Use ~보다 더 to say "more than."

How to Use

Noun + 보다 더 + adjective.

Eg: • 이 차는 저 차보다 더 빨라요 (This car is faster than that car).

Examples

i. 이 집이 저 집보다 더 커요.

ii. 이 음식이 저 음식보다 더 맛있어요.

iii.　오늘이 어제보다 더 따뜻해요.

iv. 이 책이 저 책보다 더 재미있어요.

2. Superlatives: 가장 ~ (The Most)

가장 ~ is used to express the superlative degree, meaning "the most" or "the best."

- Attach 가장 before adjectives.

How to Use

가장 + adjective.

Eg: 이 음식이 가장 맛있어요 (This food is the most delicious).

Examples

i. 이 차가 가장 빨라요.

ii. 이 음식이 가장 비싸요.

iii. 그는 우리 중에서 가장 똑똑해요.

iv. 이 책이 가장 재미있어요.

v. 봄이 가장 좋아요.

3. Expressing Preferences: ~보다 (Than)

Use ~보다 to indicate a preference or comparison.

- It is used to compare two things directly.

How to Use

Noun + 보다 + adjective.

Eg: • 저는 커피보다 차를 더 좋아해요 (I prefer tea to coffee).

Examples

i.   저는 자전거보다 자동차를 더 좋아해요.

ii.   그는 일보다 휴식을 더 원해요.

iii. 저는 이 옷이 저 옷보다 더 예뻐요.

iv. 저는 맥주보다 와인을 더 좋아해요.

v.   저는 이 영화가 저 영화보다 더 재미있어요.

4. Using 'The Least': 덜/가장 덜~ (Less/The least)

덜/가장 덜~ (Less/The least) is used to express the opposite of the superlative, meaning "less" or "the least."

How to Use

덜/가장 덜~ (Less/The least) **+ adjective.**

Eg: 이 음식이 덜 매워요 (This food is less spicy).

Examples

i. 이 일은 덜 중요해요.

ii. 그 차는 덜 빠르다.

iii.   이 영화가 덜 재미있어요.

iv.   이 커피가 덜 달아요.

v. 그 사람은 덜 똑똑해요.

IV. Exercise

1. Complete each sentence using the ~보다 더 form.

   i. 이 영화가 저 영화 _____ 재미있어요.

   ii. 오늘이 어제 _____ 더워요.

   iii. 이 음식이 저 음식 _____ 맛있어요.

   iv. 이 사람이 저 사람 _____ 똑똑해요.

   v. 나는 차보다 커피를 _____ 좋아해요.

2. Match each comparative sentence in Column A with the most appropriate response in Column B.

Column A	Column B
i. 이 집은 저 집보다 더 넓어요.	a) "네, 이 영화는 정말 흥미로워요.
ii. 이 음식이 저 음식보다 덜 매워요.	b) "맞아요. 그래서 여기서 사는 게 좋아요."
iii. 그는 우리 중에서 가장 똑똑해요.	c) "그래서 저는 이 차를 샀어요."
iv. 이 차가 저 차보다 더 빨라요.	d) "아, 그럼 이 음식을 먹어볼게요."
v. 이 영화가 가장 재미있어요.	e) "그는 정말 지식이 많아요."

3. Convert the following phrases to express preferences using ~보다.

   Eg: 차 / 자전거 → <u>저는 차보다 자전거를 더 좋아해요.</u>

   i. 휴식 / 일 → _____

   ii. 와인 / 맥주 → _____

   iii.   영화 / 책 → _____

   iv.   옷 / 신발 → _____

4. Complete each sentence using the correct comparative, superlative, or preference pattern from the Word Bank.

> 더, 보다, 가장, 덜, 좋아해요, 편안해요, 비싸요,
> 피곤해요, 빠릅니다

   i. 이 호텔은 저 호텔 _____ _____. (more comfortable)

   ii. 나는 맥주 _____ 와인을 더 _____. (than, like)

   iii.   이 차는 우리 중에서 _____ _____. (the fastest)

   iv.   이 옷이 저 옷 _____ _____. (more expensive than)

   v. 자전거 타는 것이 걷기 _____ _____. (less tiring than)

5. Rearrange the words to form correct sentences.

Eg: 더 / 그는 / 똑똑해요 / 나

<u>그는 나보다 더 똑똑해요.</u>

i. 가장 / 이 영화가 / 재미있어요

_____

ii. 보다 / 저는 / 차를 / 버스 / 더 좋아해요

_____

iii. 덜 / 이 커피가 / 저 커피 / 달아요/ 보다

_____

iv. 비싸요 / 이 가방이 / 모든 가방 중에서 / 가장

_____

Chapter- 14
EXPRESSING EMOTIONS

I. Vocabulary

기쁨	joy
슬픔	sadness
화	anger
놀라움	surprise
사랑	love
두려움	fear
불안	anxiety
질투	jealousy
행복	happiness
외로움	loneliness
만족	satisfaction
실망	disappointment
긴장	nervousness
후회	regret
걱정	worry
감사	gratitude
미안함/사과	apology
자부심	pride
용기	courage

욕심	greed
즐거움	pleasure
분노	rage
부러움	envy
우울함	depression
편안함	comfort
혼란	confusion
자신감	confidence
희망	hope
절망	despair
아쉬움	frustration
상처	hurt
신뢰	trust

Expressions

감사해요	I am grateful.
부러워요.	I am envious.
우울해요	I am depressed.
편안해요	I feel comfortable.
혼란스러워요	I am confused.
자신 있어요	I am confident.
희망해요	I hope.
절망해요	I despair.

II. Conversation

A: 요즘 기분이 어때요?
B: 조금 우울해요.
일이 잘 안 돼서 그래요.
A: 그래요? 저도 기분이 안 좋아요.
친구와 다퉈서 화나요.
B: 그렇군요.
저는 행복하고 싶어요.
A: 저도 그래요. 우리 같이
기분 전환을 할까요?

How have you been feeling these days?
I feel a bit depressed.
Things are not going well.
Really? I also feel bad. I had an
argument with a friend, so I am angry.
I see.
I want to be happy.
Me too.
Shall we do something to cheer up?

III. Grammar

1. Feeling Verbs: 기쁘다, 슬프다, 화나다

These verbs express direct emotions.

How to Use

Subject + 기뻐요/슬퍼요/화나요.

Eg: • 저는 기뻐요 **(I am happy).**
• 그는 슬퍼요 **(He is sad).**

Example

i. 저는 기뻐요.
ii. 그녀는 슬퍼요.
iii. 그는 정말 화나요.
iv. 오늘은 기쁜 날이에요.
v. 그 소식을 듣고 슬펐어요.

2. Expressing Emotions: ~아서/어서 (Because of, Due to)

Use ~아서/어서 to explain why you feel a certain way.

How to Use

Verb/Adjective stem + ~아서/어서.

Eg: • 기뻐서 (because I am happy),
   • 슬퍼서 (because I am sad).

Example

i. 좋은 소식을 들어서 기뻐요.

ii. 친구가 떠나서 슬퍼요.

iii. 일이 잘 안 돼서 화나요.

iv. 시험에 합격해서 기뻐요.

v. 날씨가 나빠서 슬퍼요.

3. Describing States: ~고 있다 (Ongoing State)

Use ~고 있다 to describe ongoing emotional states.

How to Use

Verb stem + ~고 있다.

Eg: • 기뻐하고 있다 (being happy),
   • 슬퍼하고 있다 (being sad).

Example

i. 그는 지금 웃고 있어요.

ii. 저는 지금 울고 있어요.

iii. 그녀는 화를 내고 있어요.

iv. 아이가 놀라고 있어요.

v. 우리는 지금 행복해하고 있어요.

4. Using "Want to Feel": ~고 싶다 (Want to)

Use ~고 싶다 to express a desire to feel a certain emotion.

How to Use

Verb stem + ~고 싶다.

Eg: • 행복하고 싶다 (want to be happy).

Example

i. 저는 행복하고 싶어요.

ii. 그는 기뻐하고 싶어요.

iii. 우리는 더 이상 슬프고 싶지 않아요.

iv. 그녀는 화나고 싶지 않아요.

v. 나는 사랑받고 싶어요.

IV. Exercise

1. Complete the sentences using the appropriate feeling verbs.

i. 시험에 합격해서 _____. (happy)

ii. 친구와 헤어져서 _____. (sad)

iii. 차가 막혀서 _____. (angry)

iv. 선물을 받아서 _____. (happy)

v. 나쁜 소식을 들어서 _____. (sad)

2. Translate the following sentences into Korean

i. I am happy because of the good news.

ii. She is crying because she is sad.

iii. He is getting angry right now.

iv. I want to be happy.

v. I am sad because my friend left.

3. Match each emotion with the correct reason.

Column A	Column B
i. 슬퍼요	a) 좋은 소식을 들어서
ii. 기뻐요	b) 일이 잘 안 돼서
iii. 화나요	c) 친구와 다퉈서
iv. 놀라요	d) 갑자기 소리를 들어서
v. 행복해요	e) 사랑하는 사람과 함께 있어서

4. Use ~고 있다 to describe the ongoing emotions in the following sentences.

Eg: 그는 지금 웃다.

<u>그는 지금 웃고 있어요.</u>

i. 저는 지금 울다.

_____

ii. 그녀는 화를 내다.

_____

iii. 아이가 놀라다.

_____

iv. 우리는 지금 행복해하다.

_____

5. Rearrange the words to form correct sentences.

i. 기뻐요 / 좋은 소식을 / 들어서

_____

ii. 슬퍼요 / 일이 / 잘 / 안 돼서

_____

iii. 싫어요 / 저는 / 행복하고

_____

iv. 있어요 / 지금/ 그는 / 웃고

_____

v. 화나요 / 차가 / 막혀서

_____

Chapter- 15

DAILY ROUTINES AND HABITS

I. Vocabulary

일어나기	waking up
씻기	washing
세수	face washing
샤워	shower
양치질	brushing teeth
아침 식사	breakfast
점심	lunch
저녁 식사	dinner
간식	snack
일하기	working
공부	studying
운동	exercising
청소	cleaning
설거지	washing dishes
빨래	doing laundry
옷 입기	dressing up
머리 감기	washing hair
머리 빗기	combing hair
장보기	grocery shopping
쓰레기 버리기	taking out the trash
요리	cooking

식사 준비	meal preparation
전화하기	making a phone call
이메일 확인	checking emails
출근	going to work
퇴근	getting off work
버스 타기	taking the bus
지하철 타기	taking the subway
걷기	walking
책 읽기	reading a book
텔레비전 보기	watching TV
휴식	resting
잠자기	sleeping

Expressions

아침을 먹어야 해요	I have to eat breakfast.
운동할 필요가 있어요	I need to exercise.
출근해야 해요.	I have to go to work.
퇴근 후에는 쉬는 게 좋아요	It's good to rest after work.
저녁을 만들어야 해요	I have to cook dinner.
책을 읽는 게 좋아요	It's good to read a book.
빨래할 필요가 있어요	I need to do laundry.
양치질하는 게 중요해요	Brushing teeth is important.
식사 준비를 해야 해요	I have to prepare meals.
청소하는 게 좋아요	It's good to clean.
일찍 자는 게 좋아요	It's good to sleep early.

II. Conversation

A: 아침에 일어나서 뭐 해요?

B: 저는 일어나자마자 세수를 하고 양치질해요.

A: 아침을 꼭 먹어야 해요. 건강에 좋아요.

B: 맞아요. 그래서 저는 매일 아침을 먹으려고 해요.

A: 운동도 자주 해요?

B: 네, 건강을 위해 매일 운동할 필요가 있어요.

What do you do after waking up in the morning?

As soon as I wake up, I wash my face and brush my teeth.

You must eat breakfast. It's good for your health.

Right. That's why I try to eat breakfast every day.

Do you exercise often, too?

Yes, I need to exercise every day for my health.

III. Grammar

1. Obligation: ~아/어야 하다 (Must, Have to)

Used to express something that one must or has to do.

How to Use

Verb stem + ~아/어야 하다.

Eg:• 가다 → 가야 하다 (have to go).

Examples

i. 저는 일찍 일어나야 해요.

ii. 출근하기 전에 씻어야 해요.

iii. 아침을 먹어야 해요.

iv. 운동을 해야 해요.

v. 오늘은 청소를 해야 해요.

2. Necessity: ~필요하다 (Need to)

Used to express the necessity of doing something.

How to Use

Verb stem + ~할 필요가 있다.

Eg: 운동하다 → 운동할 필요가 있다 (need to exercise).

Examples

i. 저는 오늘 빨래할 필요가 있어요.

ii. 집에 가기 전에 기장을 봐야 할 필요가 있어요.

iii. 더 건강해지려면 운동할 필요가 있어요.

iv. 이 이메일을 확인할 필요가 있어요.

v. 내일의 회의를 위해 준비할 필요가 있어요.

3. Suggestion: ~하는 게 좋다 (It's Good to Do)

Used to suggest a good or preferable action.

How to Use

Verb stem + ~하는 게 좋다.

Eg: 쉬다 → 쉬는 게 좋다 (it's good to rest).

Examples

i. 일찍 자는 게 좋아요.

ii. 아침에 운동하는 게 좋아요.

iii. 식사 후에 양치질하는 게 좋아요.

iv. 주말에는 휴식하는 게 좋아요.

v. 매일 책을 읽는 게 좋아요.

4. Expressing a Habit: ~곤 하다 (Tend to)

Used to express habits or actions done regularly.

How to Use

Verb stem + ~곤 하다

Eg: 운동하다 → 운동하곤 하다 (tend to exercise).

Examples

i. 저는 아침마다 산책하곤 해요.

ii. 그는 저녁에 TV를 보곤 해요.

iii. 그녀는 주말마다 청소하곤 해요.

iv. 저는 잠자기 전에 책을 읽곤 해요.

v. 그는 점심 후에 커피를 마시곤 해요.

IV. Exercise

1. Complete the sentences using the ~아/어야 하다 form.

    i. 아침에 일찍 _____ 해요. (wake up)

    ii. 오늘 저녁은 이곳에서 _____ 해요. (cook)

    iii. 학교에 가기 전에 숙제를 _____ 해요. (finish)

    iv. 건강을 위해 매일 _____ 해요. (exercise)

    v. 집에 들어오기 전에 장을 _____ 해요. (buy groceries)

2. Choose the best phrase to complete the sentence. (Using ~하는 게 좋다)

    i. 아침에 일찍 _____ 게 좋아요. (wake up)

    ii. 식사 후에 양치질 _____ 게 좋아요. (brush teeth)

    iii. 저녁에 잠자기 전에 책을 _____ 게 좋아요. (read)

    iv. 일찍 _____ 게 좋아요. (sleep)

    v. 운동을 _____ 게 좋아요. (do)

3. Rearrange the Words (Necessity ~필요하다)

    i. 필요가 있어요 / 방을 / 청소할

    _____

    ii. 더 / 공부할 / 필요가 있어요

    _____

iii. 필요가 있어요 / 이메일을 / 확인할

_____

iv. 필요가 있어요 / 내일의 회의를 / 준비할

_____

v. 운동할 / 필요가 있어요 / 건강을 위해

_____

4. Match each daily routine with the appropriate habit expressed using ~곤 하다.

Column A	Column B
i. 저는 아침마다 공원에서	a) TV를 보곤 해요.
ii. 그는 저녁에 가족들과	b) 산책을 하곤 해요.
iii. 그녀는 주말에 집을	c) 커피를 마시곤 해요.
iv. 우리는 매일 점심 후에	d) 청소하곤 해요.
v. 나는 자기 전에 좋아하는	e) 책을 읽곤 해요.

5. Read the passage and answer the following questions.

민지는 아침에 일찍 일어나서 하루를 시작해요. 일어나자마자 세수를 하고, 아침 식사를 준비해야 해요. 건강을 위해 매일 아침 운동을 하는 게 좋아서, 그녀는 운동을 하곤 해요. 운동을 마친 후에는 아침을 먹고, 양치질을 해요.

아침 9시까지 회사에 가야 해서 빨리 옷을 갈아입고, 출근 준비를 해야 해요.

회사에서는 점심시간 전에 중요한 이메일을 확인할 필요가 있어요. 점심 식사를 마친 후에는 가끔 산책을 하곤 해요. 퇴근 후에는 집에 와서 저녁 식사를 준비해야 해요. 저녁 식사 후에는 설거지를 하고, 방을 청소할 필요가 있어요. 하루를 마무리하기 전에, 민지는 잠자기 전에 책을 읽곤 해요. 일찍 자는 게 건강에 좋다고 생각해서, 그녀는 보통 10시쯤 잠자리에 들어요.

A. Complete the sentences based on the passage.

i. 민지는 아침에 일어나자마자 _____ 하고, 아침 식사를 준비해야 해요. (wash face)

ii. 건강을 위해 민지는 매일 아침에 _____ 을/를 해요. (exercise)

iii. 회사에서는 점심시간 전에 중요한 _____ 을/를 확인할 필요가 있어요. (emails)

iv. 퇴근 후에는 집에 와서 _____ 을/를 준비해야 해요. (dinner)

v. 잠자기 전에, 민지는 _____ 을/를 읽곤 해요. (book)

B. Decide whether the following statements are True or False.

i. 민지는 아침에 일어나자마자 운동을 해요.

ii. 민지는 점심시간 전에 이메일을 확인할 필요가 있어요.

iii. 민지는 저녁 식사 후에 보통 설거지를 하지 않아요.

iv. 민지는 잠자기 전에 책을 읽곤 해요.

v. 민지는 보통 밤 12시쯤 잠자리에 들어요.

Chapter- 16
BODY AND HEALTH

I. Vocabulary

머리	head
얼굴	face
눈	eye
눈썹	eyebrow
코	nose
입	mouth
입술	lips
이/치아	tooth/teeth
귀	ear
턱	chin
목	neck
어깨	shoulder
팔	arm
팔꿈치	clbow
손	hand
손목	wrist
손가락	finger
손톱	fingernail
가슴	chest
배	stomach
허리	waist

등	back
엉덩이	hip
다리	leg
무릎	knee
발	foot
발목	ankle
발가락	toe
피부	skin
근육	muscle
심장	heart
아프다	to be in pain
부었다	to be swollen
다쳤다	to be hurt

Expressions

통증이 있다	to have pain
두통이 있다	to have a headache
피가 나다	to bleed
근육통이 있다	to have muscle pain
열이 나다	to have a fever
땀이 나다	to sweat
소리가 들리다	to hear sounds
느낌이 이상하다	to feel strange
피부가 건조하다	to have dry skin
심장이 빨리 뛰다	heart beats fast

II. Conversation

A: 요즘 몸이 어때요?   How is your body feeling these days?

B: 팔과 어깨가 아파요.   My arms and shoulders hurt.

일 때문에 그런 것 같아요.   I think it's because of work.

A: 다리도 아프지 않아요?   Aren't your legs hurting too?

B: 네, 다리도 아파요.   Yes, my legs hurt, too.

운동 때문에 그래요.   It's because of exercise.

A: 병원에 가서 진료를   You should go to see a doctor and

받는 게 좋겠어요.   get a check-up.

B: 네, 치료를 받아야 할   Yes, I think I need to get

것 같아요.   the treatment.

III. Grammar

1. ~에서 (At, In, From)

~에서 is used to indicate a location or origin of an action, similar to "at," "in," or "from" in English.

How to Use

Place + 에서 + verb.

Eg: • 병원에서 치료를 받아요 **(I receive treatment at the hospitalclinic)**

Examples

i. 병원에서 치료를 받아요.

ii. 집에서 쉬고 있어요.

iii. 공원에서 운동해요.

iv. 이 약은 약국에서 샀어요.

v. 도서관에서 책을 읽어요.

2. ~과/와 (With, And)

~과/와 is used to connect nouns, like "and" or "with" in English.

How to Use

Noun + 과/와 + Noun.

Eg: • 저는 친구와 함께 있어요 **(I am with a friend).**

Examples

i. 친구와 병원에 갔어요.

ii. 의사와 상담했어요.

iii. 엄마와 함께 있어요.

iv. 손과 팔이 아파요.

v. 눈과 코가 가려워요.

3. ~도 (Also, Too)

~도 is used to indicate inclusion, like "also" or "too" in English.

How to Use

Noun + 도.

Eg: • 다리도 아파요 (My legs hurt, too).

Examples

i. 다리도 아파요.

ii. 손도 부었어요.

iii. 어깨도 불편해요.

iv. 피부도 가려워요.

v. 허리도 이상해요.

4. ~때문에 (Because of/Due to)

~때문에 is used to indicate the cause or reason, similar to "because of" or "due to" in English.

How to Use

Noun + 때문에 + Result.

Eg: • 감기 때문에 병원에 갔어요

(I went to the clinic because of a cold).

Examples

i. 감기 때문에 약을 먹어요.

ii. 일 때문에 어깨가 아파요.

iii. 운동 때문에 다리가 아파요.

iv. 부상 때문에 병원에 갔어요.

v. 감기 때문에 집에 있어요.

IV. Exercise

1. Scenario-Based Fill in the Blanks (Using ~때문에)

Scenario: You are at the doctor's office explaining your symptoms. Complete each sentence to explain your symptoms using the ~때문에 (because of) pattern.

i. 어제 운동을 많이 해서 _____ 때문에 다리가 아파요. **(exercise)**

ii. 추운 _____ 때문에 목이 아파요. **(cold weather)**

iii.   _____ 때문에 두통이 생겼어요. **(stress)**

iv. 무거운 가방을 오래 들고 있어서 _____ 때문에 팔이 아파요. **(heavy bag)**

v. 화학 제품을 사용한 후에 _____ 때문에 피부가 가려워요. **(chemical products)**

2. Problem Solving (Using ~이/가 아프다)

Scenario: You are a nurse and need to understand a patient's pain areas based on their complaints. Read each description and choose the correct body part experiencing pain.

i. "책상에 팔꿈치를 너무 오래 대고 있었어요. 이제 여기가 아파요."

a) 머리

b) 팔꿈치

c) 다리

ii. "운동을 너무 많이 했어요. 특히 발목이 너무 아파요."

a) 발목

b) 손목

c) 어깨

iii. "무거운 책을 오래 들고 있어서 여기가 아파요."

a) 손

b) 허리

c) 팔

iv. "찬 음식을 먹고 나서 여기가 좀 아파요."

a) 이

b) 입

c) 배

v. "갑자기 너무 많이 걸었더니 여기가 아파요."

a) 손가락

b) 다리

c) 손목

3. Match each symptom with its possible cause using ~때문에.

Symptoms	Causes
i. 피부가 가려워요	a) 컴퓨터를 오래 사용했어요.
ii. 허리가 아파요	b) 새로운 화장품을 썼어요.
iii. 다리가 아파요	c) 오래 걸었어요.
iv. 눈이 아파요	d) 무거운 물건을 들었어요.
v. 손목이 아파요	e) 계속 글씨를 많이 썼어요.

4. Translate the Symptoms (Using Various Patterns)

i. I have to go to the clinic because of my headache.

ii. My wrist and fingers hurt because of computer work.

iii. I exercise at the park every morning, and my friend joins me, too.

iv. My back hurts because of lifting heavy objects.

v. My eyes are also tired from reading.

5. Read the passage and answer the questions based on the descriptions.

수진이는 어제 운동을 너무 많이 해서 다리와 발목이 아파요. 오늘 아침에는 일어나서 팔도 조금 아팠어요. 어제 운동 후에는 공원에서 친구와 이야기를 하다가 넘어졌어요. 그래서 무릎도 조금 다쳤어요. 친구는 그와 같이 병원에 가서 진료를 받는 게 좋다고 했지만, 수진이는 그냥 집에서 쉬고 싶다고 했어요.

i. 수진이의 다리와 발목이 아픈 이유는 무엇인가요?

Answer: _____

ii. 수진이는 어디에서 친구와 이야기를 했나요?

Answer: _____

iii. 수진이의 친구가 추천한 것은 무엇인가요?

Answer: _____

iv. 수진이의 다친 부위는 어디인가요?

Answer: _____

v. 수진이는 병원에 가고 싶어 하나요, 아니면 집에 있고 싶어 하나요?

Answer: _____

Chapter- 17
SEASONS AND PREFERENCES

I. Vocabulary

날씨	weather
계절	season
봄	spring
여름	summer
가을	autumn/fall
겨울	winter
맑음	clear
비	rain
눈	snow
바람	wind
습기	humidity
안개	fog
번개	lightning
태풍	typhoon
구름	cloud
온도	temperature
추위	coldness
더위	heat
장마	monsoon
햇볕	sunshine
습도	humidity
바닷바람	sea breeze

산들바람	gentle breeze
소나기	shower
기분	mood
행복	happiness
불안	anxiety
우울	depression
긴장	nervousness
걱정	worry
신남	excitement
짜증	annoyance
평화	peace
피곤함	fatigue
만족	satisfaction
설렘	anticipation
여유	leisure
피로	tiredness
보통	usually
자주	often
항상	always
가끔	sometimes
갑자기	suddenly
조금	a little
꽤	quite

매우	very
특히	especially
완전히	completely
그다지	not so much
마치	as if
즉시	immediately
서서히	gradually
여전히	still
느리게	slowly
빠르게	quickly
한편	on one hand
차분히	calmly

Expressions

날씨가 좋네요	The weather is nice
바람이 시원해요	The breeze is refreshing
비가 와서 우울해요	It's raining, so I feel down
햇볕이 따뜻해서 기분이 좋아요	The sunshine is warm, so I feel happy
더위 때문에 짜증나요	I feel annoyed because of the heat
눈이 내려서 설레요	Snow makes me feel excited
날씨가 흐려서 조금 피곤해요	The cloudy weather makes me feel tired
바람이 불어서 상쾌해요	The wind is refreshing
하늘이 맑아서 기분이 좋아요	The sky is clear, so I feel good

II. Conversation

A: 오늘 날씨가 참 좋네요!   The weather is really nice today!

B: 네, 하늘이 맑아서   Yes, the clear sky makes

기분이 좋아요.   me feel good.

A: 저는 맑은 날보다 비   I actually prefer rainy days

오는 날이 더 좋아요.   over sunny days.

B: 그렇군요. 저는 비가   Really? I feel a bit down

오면 조금 우울해져요.   when it rains.

A: 그럼, 오늘 같은 날에는   Then what do you want

뭐 하고 싶어요?   to do on a day like today?

B: 따뜻한 햇볕 아래에서   I want to take a walk in

산책하고 싶어요.   the warm sunshine.

III. Grammar

1. Expressing Reactions: ~네요

~네요 is used to express surprise, admiration, or realization about something, similar to "oh!" or "wow!" in English.

How to Use

Verb stem + ~네요.

Eg: 맑다 → 맑네요 (Oh, it's clear!)

Examples

i. 날씨가 좋네요!

ii. 바람이 시원하네요!

iii. 구름이 많네요!

iv. 오늘은 정말 덥네요!

v. 눈이 오네요!

2. Expressing Cause and Effect: ~아서/어서 (Because, So)

~아서/어서 is used to express the reason or cause for something, similar to "because" or "so" in English.

How to Use

Verb stem + ~아서/어서.

Eg: 덥다 → 더워서 (because it's hot)

Examples

i. 비가 와서 우울해요.

ii. 날씨가 추워서 집에 있고 싶어요.

iii. 햇볕이 따뜻해서 기분이 좋아요.

iv. 바람이 불어서 상쾌해요.

v. 하늘이 맑아서 기분이 좋아요.

3. Expressing Preference: ~보다 더 (More Than)

~보다 더 is used to compare things, similar to "more than" in English.

How to Use

Noun + 보다 더 + adjective.

Eg: 여름보다 더 시원해요 (Cooler than summer).

Examples

i. 겨울이 여름보다 더 추워요.

ii. 맑은 날이 비 오는 날보다 더 좋아요.

iii. 가을이 봄보다 더 시원해요.

iv. 구름 낀 날보다 맑은 날이 좋아요.

v. 비 오는 날보다 햇볕이 나는 날이 더 좋아요.

4. Expressing Frequency: ~마다 (Every)

~마다 is used to indicate repetition or frequency, similar to "every" in English.

How to Use

Noun + ~마다.

Eg: 날마다 (every day)

Examples

i. 날마다 날씨가 달라요.

ii. 봄마다 꽃이 피어요.

iii. 주말마다 비가 와요.

iv. 겨울마다 눈이 내려요.

v. 아침마다 바람이 불어요.

IV. Exercise

1. Complete each sentence using ~아서/어서 to explain the reason for each mood.

   i. 비가 와 _____ 우울해요.

   ii. 날씨가 추워_____ 집에 있고 싶어요.

   iii. 바람이 불_____ 상쾌해요.

   iv. 하늘이 맑_____ 기분이 좋아요.

   v. 너무 더워_____ 밖에 나가고 싶지 않아요.

2. Choose the correct form to complete the comparison.

i. 여름보다 겨울이 더 _____ (cold).

a) 덥다

b) 시원하다

c) 춥다

ii. 맑은 날이 비 오는 날보다 더 _____ (nice).

a) 싫다

b) 좋다

c) 슬프다

iii. 겨울보다 봄이 더 _____ (warm).

a) 춥다

b) 따뜻하다

c) 시원하다

iv. 비 오는 날보다 눈 오는 날이 더 _____ (exciting).

a) 설레다

b) 지겹다

c) 불편하다

v. 가을보다 여름이 더 _____ (hot).

a) 춥다

b) 덥다

c) 따뜻하다

3. Fill in the Blanks (Using ~네요)

i. 오늘 날씨가 정말 덥_____!

ii. 바람이 시원하_____!

iii. 구름이 많_____!

iv. 눈이 오_____!

v. 하늘이 맑_____!

4. Translate the following sentences into Korean using ~보다 더 to make comparisons.

i. Spring is warmer than winter.

ii. I like sunny days more than rainy days.

iii. Today's weather is cooler than yesterday's.

iv. Summer is hotter than autumn.

v. Clear skies are nicer than cloudy skies

5. Match the Weather with Emotions

Weather Conditions

i. 맑은 날

ii. 비 오는 날

iii. 더운 여름

iv. 눈 내리는 겨울

v. 바람이 부는 가을

Emotions

a) 기분이 좋아서 산책하고 싶어요.

b) 설레서 밖을 보고 있어요.

c) 시원해서 상쾌해요.

d) 더워서 피곤해요.

e) 우울해요.

Chapter- 18
HOBBIES AND PASTIMES

I. Vocabulary

취미	hobby
스포츠	sports
축구	soccer
농구	basketball
테니스	tennis
배드민턴	badminton
골프	golf
야구	baseball
배구	volleyball
달리기	running
자전거 타기	cycling
등산	hiking
수영	swimming
요가	yoga
체조	gymnastics
독서	reading
여행	trip/traveling
음악 감상	listening to music
사진 찍기	photography
요리	cooking
춤	dancing

노래 부르기	singing
글쓰기	writing
악기 연주	playing an instrument
영화 감상	watching movies
게임	gaming
보드 게임	board games
정원 가꾸기	gardening
자수	embroidery
명상	meditation
낚시	fishing
캠핑	camping
식물 기르기	plant care

Expressions

한 달에 한 번 해요	I do it once a month
일주일에 두 번 해요	I do it twice a week
운동을 하러 가요	I go to exercise
취미를 즐길 때	When I enjoy a hobby
친구와 같이 해요	I do it with a friend
집에서 주로 해요	I usually do it at home
산에서 등산해요	I go hiking in the mountains
연습을 많이 해요	I practice a lot
혼자 할 때가 많아요	I often do it alone
가끔 새로운 취미를 찾아요	I sometimes look for new hobbies

II. Conversation

A: 주말에 뭐 해요?

B: 저는 친구와 농구하러 공원에 가요. 당신은요?

A: 저는 가끔 등산하러 가요. 산에 갈 때 기분이 상쾌해요.

B: 등산하면서 음악도 들어요?

A: 네, 음악을 들으면서 걸으면 더 즐거워요.

What do you do on weekends?

I go to the park to play basketball with a friend. How about you?

I sometimes go hiking. I feel refreshed when I go to the mountain.

Do you also listen to music while hiking?

Yes, walking while listening to music makes it more enjoyable.

III. Grammar

1. Expressing "When": ~(으)ㄹ 때 (When)

~(으)ㄹ 때 is used to indicate when something happens.

How to Use

Verb stem + (으)ㄹ 때.

Eg: 책을 읽을 때 (when I read a book).

Examples

i. 저는 자전거를 탈 때 기분이 좋아요.

ii. 친구와 같이 농구할 때 재미있어요.

iii. 주말에 영화 볼 때 주로 팝콘을 먹어요.

iv. 등산할 때 산이 예뻐요.

v. 요리할 때 음악을 듣는 걸 좋아해요.

2. Purpose of Going: ~(으)러 가다 (To Go in Order to)

~(으)러 가다 is used to indicate going somewhere to perform a specific action.

How to Use
Verb stem + (으)러 가다.

Eg: 운동하러 가다 (to go to exercise).

Examples
i. 주말에 등산하러 산에 가요.
ii. 친구와 같이 테니스를 치러 공원에 가요.
iii. 사진을 찍으러 바다에 갔어요.
iv. 수영하러 수영장에 가요.
v. 운동하러 헬스장에 자주 가요.

3. Expressing Enjoyment of Activities: ~(으)면서 (While Doing)

~(으)면서 is used to describe doing two actions simultaneously, such as doing a hobby while enjoying another activity.

How to Use
Verb stem + ~(으)면서.

Eg: 음악을 들으면서 공부해요 (I study while listening to music).

Examples
i. 저는 산책하면서 음악을 들어요.
ii. 책을 읽으면서 커피를 마셔요.
iii. 친구와 이야기하면서 농구를 해요.

iv. 요리하면서 새로운 레시피를 생각해요.

v. TV를 보면서 운동을 해요.

4. Expressing Habitual Actions: ~(으)ㄴ 적이 있다

~(으)ㄴ 적이 있다 is used to indicate that someone has had an experience of doing something in the past, which is often used to talk about hobbies or activities done before.

How to Use

Verb stem + (으)ㄴ 적이 있다.

Eg: 골프를 해본 적이 있어요 (I have tried playing golf before).

Examples

i. 저는 캠핑을 해본 적이 있어요.

ii. 해외여행을 가본 적이 있어요.

iii. 자전거를 타본 적이 없어요.

iv. 친구와 함께 배드민턴을 쳐본 적이 있어요.

v. 요가를 해본 적이 있어요.

IV. Exercise

1. Fill in the Blanks (Using ~(으)ㄹ 때)

i. 저는 영화 _____ 즐거워요. (watch)

ii. 책을 _____ 시간이 빨리 가요. (read)

iii. 친구와 같이 수영 _____ 신나요. (swim)

iv. 요리 _____ 항상 음악을 들어요. (cook)

v. 저녁을 _____ 주로 TV를 봐요. (eat)

2. Choose the correct word to complete each sentence

i. 주말에 친구와 _____ 공원에 가요.

a) 운동하러

b) 운동할 때

c) 운동하면서

ii. 사진을 찍으_____ 산에 갔어요.

a) 고

b) 때

c) 러

iii. 매주 금요일 저녁에 _____ 강에 가요.

a) 낚시하러

b) 낚시할 때

c) 낚시하면서

iv. 새 책을 _____ 도서관에 가요.

a) 찾을 때

b) 찾으러

c) 찾으면

v. 저녁마다 산책하_____ 공원에 가요.

a) 로

b) 때

c) 러

3. Change to the Correct Grammar Form

Convert each sentence below to the correct grammar form as instructed.

A. Change to ~(으)ㄹ 때 (When)

i. 저는 음악을 듣다. (Change: "When I listen to music, I feel relaxed.")

_____

ii. 친구와 테니스를 치다. (Change: "It's fun when I play tennis with my friend.")

_____

iii. 요리하다, 저는 항상 레시피를 본다. (Change: "When I cook, I always check the recipe.")

_____

B. Change to ~(으)러 가다 (To go to do something)

i. 저는 운동하다 헬스장에 갔어요. (Change: "I went to the gym to exercise.")

_____

ii. 친구와 같이 자전거 타다 공원에 갔어요. (Change to: "I went to the park with my friend to ride bikes.")

_____

iii. 산책하다 공원에 갔어요. (Change to: "I went to the park to take a walk.")

_____

C. Change to ~(으)면서 (While doing)

i. 저는 독서하다 음악을 들어요. (Change to: "I listen to music while reading.")

_____

ii. 친구와 산책하다 이야기해요. (Change to: "I talk with my friend while walking.")

_____

iii. 요리하다 새로운 레시피를 생각해요. (Change to: "I think of new recipes while cooking.")

_____

Chapter- 19
TRAVEL AND ADVENTURE

I. Vocabulary

서울	Seoul
경복궁	Gyeongbokgung Palace
창덕궁	Changdeokgung Palace
북촌 한옥마을	Bukchon Hanok Village
남산	Namsan
한강	Han River
명동	Myeongdong
홍대	Hongdae
인사동	Insadong
제주도	Jeju Island
한라산	Hallasan Mountain
서귀포	Seogwipo
부산	Busan
해운대	Haeundae Beach
광안리	Gwangalli Beach
자갈치 시장	Jagalchi Market
경주	Gyeongju
안동	Andong
설악산	Seoraksan Mountain
울릉도	Ulleungdo Island
속초	Sokcho
전주 한옥마을	Jeonju Hanok Village
동대문	Dongdaemun

남대문 시장	Namdaemun Market
서울 타워	Seoul Tower
롯데월드	Lotte World
경주 불국사	Bulguksa Temple in Gyeongju
비무장지대 (DMZ)	DMZ (Demilitarized Zone)
호텔	hotel
게스트하우스	guesthouse
호스텔	hostel
펜션	pension
한옥	hanok (traditional Korean house)
캠핑장	campsite
모텔	motel
숙소	accommodation
방문객 센터	visitor center
리셉션	reception
침대	bed
욕실	bathroom
침구	bedding
짐	luggage
예약	reservation
체크인	check-in
체크아웃	check-out
식사 포함	meals included

무료 와이파이	free Wi-Fi
주차	parking
서비스	service
객실	guest room
조식	breakfast

Expressions

예약할 수 있나요?	Can I make a reservation?
체크인은 몇 시에 하나요?	What time is check-in?
어디에서 묵을 거예요?	Where will you stay?
짐을 맡길 수 있나요?	Can I store my luggage?
한옥에서 자보고 싶어요	I want to try staying in a hanok
주차장이 있나요?	Is there parking?
무료 와이파이가 있나요?	Is there free Wi-Fi?
아침 식사도 제공되나요?	Is breakfast also provided?
방이 깨끗해요	The room is clean
숙소가 마음에 들어요	I like the accommodation

II. Conversation

A: 이번 여행에서는 어디에 갈 거예요?

Where will you go on this trip?

B: 먼저 서울에서 경복궁에 가보고 싶어요. 그리고 인사동도 구경할 거예요.

First, I want to visit Gyeongbokgung Palace in Seoul. And I'll also look around Insadong.

A: 경복궁은 미리 예약하는 게 좋아요.
사람이 많거든요.
B: 그렇군요! 숙소는 한옥에서 묵어볼 거예요.
A: 와, 좋은 생각이에요. 한옥에서 자보는 것도 특별한 경험일 거예요.

It's good to reserve tickets for Gyeongbokgung Place in advance. There are many people.
Oh, I see! I'll try staying in a hanok for accommodation.
Wow, that's a great idea. Staying in a hanok will be a special experience too.

III. Grammar

1. Future Plans: ~(으)ㄹ 거예요 (Will/Going to)

~(으)ㄹ 거예요 is used to express future plans or intentions.

How to Use
Verb stem + ~(으)ㄹ 거예요.

Eg: 갈 거예요 (I will go).

Examples

i. 이번 주말에 경복궁에 갈 거예요.
ii. 내년에 제주도로 여행 갈 거예요.
iii. 호텔에서 묵을 거예요.
iv. 명동에서 쇼핑할 거예요.
v. 한옥마을에 가서 한옥에서 자볼 거예요.

2. Trying New Experiences: ~아/어 보다 (To Try Doing)

~아/어 보다 is used to indicate trying something new or experiencing something for the first time.

How to Use
Verb stem + ~아/어 보다.

Eg: 먹어 보다 (to try eating).

Examples

i. 한복을 입어 보고 싶어요.

ii. 한옥에서 자보고 싶어요.

iii.   제제주도에서 바다를 찾아가 보고 싶어요.

iv.   전주 한옥마을에 가보고 싶어요.

v. 한국 음식을 먹어 봤어요.

3. Giving Suggestions: ~는 게 좋다 (It's Good to)

~는 게 좋다 is used to make suggestions or give advice.

How to Use

Verb stem + ~는 게 좋다.

Eg: 예약하는 게 좋다 (It's good to make a reservation).

Examples

i. 유명한 곳은 미리 예약하는 게 좋아요.

ii. 날씨가 좋을 때 한강에서 산책하는 게 좋아요.

iii.   서울에 가면 남산에 가보는 게 좋아요.

iv.   제주도에서 흑돼지를 먹어 보는 게 좋아요.

v. 관광지에 갈 때 지도를 챙기는 게 좋아요.

IV. Exercise

1. Fill in the Blanks (Using ~(으)ㄹ 거예요)

i. 저는 내일 경주에 _____. (to go)

ii. 주말에 가족과 부산에서 _____. (to stay)

iii. 이번 여름에 제주도에 _____. (to visit)

iv. 여행할 때 친구와 쇼핑을 _____. (to do)

v. 명동에서 맛있는 음식을 _____. (to eat)

2. Match the following

Column A	Column B
i. 서울에 갈 때는 한복을 _____	a) 볼 거예요
ii. 제주도에 가면 흑돼지를 _____	b) 가져가는 게 좋아요
iii. 유명한 관광지라서 미리 _____	c) 입어 보고 싶어요
iv. 친구와 함께 경주에 _____	d) 묵어 보고 싶어요
v. 한옥에서 _____	e) 예약하는 게 좋아요
vi. 관광지에서 지도를 _____	f) 먹어 볼 거예요
vii. 해운대 해수욕장에서 수영을 _____	g) 해 볼 거예요
viii. 남산에서 야경을 _____	h) 가기로 했어요

3. Read the passage and answer the following questions.

Passage

미나는 이번 주말에 친구들과 함께 부산으로 여행을 갈 거예요.
그들은 해운대 해수욕장에서 수영을 하고 싶어요.
미나는 부산에 처음 가기 때문에 유명한 음식도 먹어
보고 싶어요. 특히, 부산에서 유명한 회를 먹어 보고 싶어요.

미나는 여행을 위해 미리 숙소를 예약하는 게 좋다고 생각해요. 그리고 여행 중에 지도를 챙기는 것도 중요하다고 생각해요.

Questions

i. 미나는 이번 주말에 어디로 여행을 갈 거예요?

Answer: _____

ii. 미나와 친구들은 부산에서 무엇을 하고 싶어요?

Answer: _____

iii. 미나는 부산에서 어떤 음식을 먹어 보고 싶어 해요?

Answer: _____

iv. 수영을 하고 싶어 해요?

Answer: _____

v. 미나는 여행을 위해 미리 무엇을 하는 게 좋다고 생각해요?

Answer: _____

4. Change each sentence according to the instruction provided.

i. **Original:** 저는 다음 주에 한옥에서 묵어 보고 싶어요.

Change to: ~(으)ㄹ 거예요.

Answer: _____

ii. **Original:** 친구와 같이 서울타워에 갈 거예요.

Change to: ~는 게 좋다

Answer: _____

iii. **Original:** 경복궁에서 전통 옷을 입어 볼 거예요.

Change to: ~아/어 보다.

Answer: _____

iv. **Original:** 제주도에서 바다를 볼 거예요.

Change to: ~아/어 보다.

Answer: _____

v. **Original:** 여행할 때 미리 예약하는 게 좋다.

Change to: ~(으)ㄹ 거예요.

Answer: _____

vi. **Original:** 전주 한옥마을에 가보고 싶어요.

Change to: ~는 게 좋다.

Answer: _____

Chapter- 20

I. Vocabulary

기차	train
버스	bus
지하철	subway
택시	taxi
자전거	bicycle
자동차	car
비행기	airplane
고속버스	express bus
시외버스	intercity bus
전철	metro
모노레일	monorail
여객선	passenger ship
택시 승강장	taxi stand
버스 정류장	bus stop
지하철역	subway station
주차장	parking lot
운전면허증	driver's license
고속도로	expressway/highway
지하철 노선도	subway route map
시간표	schedule
표	ticket
도착 시간	arrival time

출발 시간	departure time
요금	fare
차량	vehicle
운전	driving
차도	road
횡단보도	crosswalk
보행자	pedestrian
길	street
버스 터미널	bus terminal
전철 노선	subway line
카드 충전	card recharge

Expressions

지하철 몇 호선을 타야 해요?	Which subway line should I take?
버스는 어디에서 타요?	Where do I take the bus?
택시 요금이 얼마에요?	How much is the taxi fare?
교통이 많이 막혀요	There's a lot of traffic
길이 많이 막혔어요	The road is very crowded
출발 시간이 언제예요?	When is the departure time?
몇 시에 도착할 거예요?	What time will it arrive?
몇 호선을 타야 하나요?	Which subway line should I take?
버스 정류장이 어디에 있어요?	Where is the bus stop?
주차할 곳이 없어요	There's no place to park
교통카드로 결제할 수 있어요?	Can I pay with a transportation card?
이 버스는 어디까지 가요?	How far does this bus go?

II. Conversation

A: 서울에서 부산까지 어떻게 갈 거예요?

B: 저는 기차나 고속버스를 타고 갈 거예요. 시간이 얼마나 걸려요?

A: 기차로는 약 세 시간 정도 걸려요. 고속버스는 더 오래 걸려요.

B: 그럼, 기차로 가는 게 좋겠네요. 표는 미리 예약해야 해요?

A: 네, 주말에는 사람이 많으니 미리 예약하는 게 좋아요.

How will you get from Seoul to Busan?

I'll take either the train or the express bus. How long does it take?

By train, it takes about three hours. The express bus takes longer.

B: Then it's better to go by train. Should I reserve a ticket in advance?

A: Yes, it's good to reserve in advance because there are a lot of people on weekends.

III. Grammar

1. Expressing "Either...or…": (이)나

(이)나 is used to indicate options, meaning "or."

How to Use

Noun + (이)나 (with 이 for words ending in consonants, 나 for vowels).

Eg: 버스나 지하철 (bus or subway)

Examples

i. 저는 버스나 지하철을 타요.

ii. 기차나 고속버스를 타고 가세요.

iii. 택시나 자전거로 갈 수 있어요.

iv. 자동차나 전철을 타고 출발해요.

v. 공항까지 버스나 지하철을 타고 가요.

2. From Place to Place: ~에서-까지 (From…to)

~에서-까지 is used to indicate the starting and ending

points of travel, meaning "from…to."

How to Use
Place + 에서 (starting point) + Place + 까지 (ending point).

Eg: 서울에서 부산까지 (from Seoul to Busan)

Examples

i. 서울에서 부산까지 기차로 가요.

ii. 집에서 회사까지 자전거로 가요.

iii. 인천에서 제주도까지 비행기로 가요.

iv. 고속도로를 타고 서울에서 대전까지 가요.

v. 역에서 호텔까지 걸어갈 수 있어요.

3. Expressing Duration: ~동안 (For/Duration)

~동안 is used to express how long something lasts, meaning "for" a

certain amount of time.

How to Use

Time period + 동안.

Eg: 두 시간 동안 (for two hours)

Examples

i. 버스를 두 시간 동안 타야 해요.

ii. 지하철을 한 시간 동안 타요.

iii. 비행기로 세 시간 동안 가요.

iv. 운전을 다섯 시간 동안 했어요.

v. 열차를 네 시간 동안 타고 갈 거예요.

IV. Exercise

1. Fill in the Blanks (Using ~(이)나 and ~에서-까지)

i. 저는 학교 _____ 집까지 버스를 타요.

ii. 서울에서 인천공항 _____ 택시를 타고 갈 거예요.

iii. 서울에서는 지하철 _____ 버스를 이용할 수 있어요.

iv. 오늘 교통이 복잡해서 자전거 _____ 지하철을 생각 중이에요.

v. 역 _____ 호텔까지 택시로 가면 빨라요.

2. Match the Statement with the Correct Ending

Column A	Column B
i. 서울에서 부산까지	a) 지하철을 타면 편리해요
ii. 공항에서 호텔까지	b) 기차로 가면 빠르게 도착해요
iii. 전철이나	c) 택시를 타는 게 편해요
iv. 교통이 복잡할 때는	d) 걸어서 갈 수 있어요
v. 서울에서는 버스나	e) 지하철을 탈 수 있어요

3. Change the Grammar Pattern

Instructions: Each sentence below uses a specific grammar pattern. Change each sentence according to the instruction provided, using the correct form as indicated. This will help you practice switching between the grammar patterns (이)나 (or), ~에서-까지 (from…to), and ~동안 (for/duration).

i. Original: 저는 서울에서 부산까지 기차로 갈 거예요.

Change to: 동안 to express how long it will take (3 hours).

Answer: _____

ii. Original: 저는 버스나 지하철을 타요.

Change to: ~에서-까지 to describe a route from "home to work."

Answer: _____

iii. Original: 친구와 함께 공항까지 택시를 타고 갔어요.

Change to: ~동안 to show the duration (45 minutes).

Answer: _____

iv. Original: 학교에서 도서관까지 걸어갔어요.

Change to: ~(이)나 to describe an alternative way to travel (bus or walk).

Answer: _____

v. Original: 저는 한 시간 동안 자전거를 타고 산책을 했어요.

Change to: ~에서-까지 to describe a route from "park to home."

Answer: _____

4. Read a passage and answer the following questions.

Passage

지수는 이번 주말에 친구들과 함께 서울에서 부산까지 여행을 갈 거예요. 그들은 서울역에서 고속열차를 타고 부산역까지 갈 거예요. 기차로는 약 두 시간 반 걸려요. 부산에 도착한 후, 지수와 친구들은 택시나 버스를 타고 해운대 해수욕장까지 가기로 했어요. 해운대에서 하루 동안 시간을 보낸 후, 그들은 다시 기차를 타고 서울로 돌아올 계획이에요. 지수는 교통이 복잡할 때는 택시보다 버스를 타는 게 좋다고 생각해요.

Questions

i. 지수와 친구들은 어떤 교통수단을 이용해 서울에서 부산까지 갈 예정인가요?

Answer: _____

ii. 부산까지 가는 기차는 얼마나 걸리나요?

Answer: _____

iii. 부산에 도착한 후, 해운대까지 가기 위해 그들이 선택할 수 있는 교통수단은 무엇인가요?

Answer: _____

iv. 지수는 교통이 복잡할 때 어떤 교통수단이 더 좋다고 생각하나요?

Answer: _____

v. 해운대에서 시간을 얼마나 보낼 예정인가요?

Answer: _____

Chapter- 21
SHOPPING AND BARGAINING

I. Vocabulary

사과	apple
바나나	banana
포도	grape
오렌지	orange
딸기	strawberry
수박	watermelon
배	pear
복숭아	peach
파인애플	pineapple
키위	kiwi
멜론	melon
귤	tangerine
자몽	grapefruit
쌀	rice
빵	bread
우유	milk
커피	coffee
주스	juice
달걀	egg
고기	meat
김치	kimchi
라면	ramen

생선	fish
밥	cooked rice
국수	noodles
소고기	beef
돼지고기	pork
닭고기	chicken
야채	vegetables
돈	money
가격	price
할인	discount
세일	sale
값	cost
거스름돈	change
지폐	bill (paper money)
동전	coin
지갑	wallet
현금	cash
신용카드	credit card
영수증	receipt
카드 결제	card payment
현금 결제	cash payment

Counter Nouns

한 개	one (item)
두 개	two (items)
세 개	three (items)
네 개	four (items)
한 잔	one (cup)
두 잔	two (cups)
세 잔	three (cups)
네 잔	four (cups)
한 마리	one (animal)
두 마리	two (animals)
세 마리	three (animals)
한 병	one (bottle)
두 병	two (bottles)
세 병	three (bottles)

Expressions

이거 얼마예요?	How much is this?
할인 받을 수 있어요?	Can I get a discount?
현금으로 결제할게요	I'll pay in cash
카드로 결제해 주세요	Please pay with a card
거스름돈 주세요	Please give me the change
다섯 개 주세요	Please give me five items
총 얼마예요?	How much is the total?
영수증 필요해요?	Do you need a receipt?

II. Conversation

A: 안녕하세요.

사과 세 개 주세요.

B: 네, 여기 있습니다.

총 가격은 천오백 원이에요.

A: 음… 조금 더 싸게

해 줄 수 있어요?

B: 알겠습니다. 천이백

원에 드릴게요.

A: 감사합니다. 오렌지

두 개도 사고 싶어요.

B: 네, 오렌지 두 개는

천 원이에요.

Hello.

Please give me three apples.

Sure, here you go.

The total cost is 1,500 won.

Hmm… Can you make it

a bit cheaper?

Okay, I'll give it to you

for 1,200 won.

Thank you. Also, I'd like to

buy two oranges.

Sure, two oranges are

1,000 won.

III. Grammar

1. Counting Objects: Noun + (Counter) + Number + 주세요

Use Noun + (Counter) + Number + 주세요 to request a specific

quantity of an item.

How to Use

Noun + Counter + Number + 주세요

Eg: 사과 세 개 주세요 **(Please give me three apples).**

Examples

i. 사과 다섯 개 주세요.

ii. 물 두 병 주세요.

iii. 빵 세 개 주세요.

iv. 커피 한 잔 주세요.

v. 계란 열 개 주세요.

2. Expressing Preference: ~고 싶다 (To Want to)

Use ~고 싶다 to express a desire or preference for something.

How to Use

Verb stem + 고 싶다

Eg: 사고 싶어요 **(I want to buy).**

Examples

i. 사과를 사고 싶어요.

ii. 저렴한 음식을 먹고 싶어요.

iii. 이 가방을 사고 싶어요.

iv. 우유 한 병을 사고 싶어요.

v. 할인된 물건을 사고 싶어요.

3. Requesting Discount or Lower Price: (~ 가격) 좀 깎아 주세요

~가격 좀 깎아 주세요 is a polite way to ask for a discount. Use this when negotiating a lower price, particularly at markets.

How to Use

Item + (~ 가격) 좀 깎아 주세요.

Eg: 사과 가격 좀 깎아 주세요. **(Please give me discount on apples.)**

Examples

i. 이거 가격 좀 깎아 주세요.

ii. 신발 가격 좀 깎아 주세요.

iii. 포도 가격 좀 깎아 주세요.

iv. 가격 좀 깎아 주세요.

v. 떡볶이 좀 싸게 해 주세요..

IV. Exercise

1. Fill in the Blanks with the Correct Counter

i. 사과 세 _____ 주세요.

ii. 친구 두 _____ 을 만날 거예요.

iii. 물 다섯 _____을 사고 싶어요.

iv. 강아지 한 _____ 를 키우고 있어요.

v. 책 네 _____ 을 사려고 해요.

2. Match each item in Column A with the correct counter in Column B.

Column A	Column B
i. 물	a) 마리
ii. 치킨	b) 명
iii. 사람	c) 병
iv. 수박	d) 권
v. 잡지	e) 개

3. Choose the correct counter for each item.

i. 배 다섯 _____ 사려고 해요. (five bunches of pears)

a) 개

b) 병

c) 권

ii. 친구 두 _____ 만났어요. (two friends)

a) 명

b) 병

c) 마리

iii. 콜라 세 _____ 주세요. (three bottles of cola)

a) 개

b) 병

c) 권

iv. 책 네 _____ 빌렸어요. (four books)

a) 개

b) 마리

c) 권

v. 강아지 한 _____ 키우고 있어요. (one dog)

a) 마리

b) 개

c) 명

4. Change the Grammar Pattern

Instructions: Each sentence below uses a specific grammar pattern or phrase. Change each sentence according to the instruction provided, using the correct form as indicated. This exercise will help you practice switching between different expressions used in a shopping or counting context.

i. **Original:** 사과 두 개 주세요.

Change to: Ask for three apples instead of two.

Answer: _____

ii. **Original:** 물 네 병을 사고 싶어요.

Change to: Ask how much four bottles of water cost using 얼마예요?

Answer: _____

iii. **Original:** 친구 세 명을 만났어요.

Change to: Describe meeting five friends instead of three.

Answer: _____

iv. **Original:** 치킨 한 마리 주세요.

Change to: Use 좀 깎아 주세요 **to request a discount on one whole chicken.**

Answer: _____

v. **Original:** 책 세 권을 읽었어요.

Change to: Describe reading four books using the correct counter for books.

Answer: _____

vi. **Original:** 수박 두 개 주세요.

Change to: Ask for three watermelons instead of two.

Answer: _____

Chapter- 22

MAKING PLANS WITH FRIENDS

I. Vocabulary

약속	plan
초대	invitation
예약	reservation
모임	gathering
파티	party
일정	schedule
시간	time
날짜	date
장소	place
친구	friend
선물	gift
기념일	anniversary
만남	meeting
축하	celebration
행사	event
계획	plan
행복한	happy
기쁜	joyful
긴장된	nervous
편안한	comfortable
확실한	certain
준비된	prepared

신나는	exciting
고마운	grateful
바쁜	busy
바라는	wishing for
만족스러운	satisfied
기대되는	expecting
달력	calendar
메모	note
메시지	message
전송	send

Expressions

약속을 잡다	To make plans
시간이 있나요?	Do you have time?
같이 가실래요?	Would you like to go together?
언제 만날까요?	When shall we meet?
초대해 주셔서 감사합니다	Thank you for the invitation
준비가 됐나요?	Are you ready?
확인해 주세요	Please confirm
일정을 정합시다	Let's set the schedule
기대돼요	I'm looking forward to it
정말 기대돼요	I'm really excited
미리 예약할게요	I'll reserve in advance
무슨 일이 있나요?	Do you have something going on?

II. Conversation

A: 이번 주말에 친구들을 초대할까요?

Shall we invite our friends this weekend?

B: 좋아요! 근데, 장소는 어디로 할까요?

Sounds good! But, where shall we do it?

A: 우리 집에서 하기로 했어요. 다들 편하게 올 수 있을 거예요.

We decided to have it at my house. Everyone can come conveniently.

B: 그럼, 제가 선물을 준비할게요. 시간은 언제로 정할까요?

Then, I'll prepare a gift. What time should we set?

A: 오후 3시로 정해요. 모두 기대할 거예요!

Let's set it for 3 PM. Everyone will be looking forward to it!

III. Grammar

1. Making Suggestions: (으)ㄹ까요? (Shall we? / Should we?)

(으)ㄹ까요? is used to make suggestions or ask if the other person would like to do something.

How to Use

Verb stem + (으)ㄹ까요?

Eg: 만날까요? (Shall we meet?)

Examples

i. 이번 주말에 만날까요?

ii. 기념일에 같이 식사할까요?

iii.   친구들을 초대할까요?

iv.   이 장소에서 만날까요?

v. 약속을 내일로 정할까요?

2. Expressing Circumstances: ~는데/~은데

~는데/~은데 is used to give background information, add context, or explain circumstances, often as a lead-in to a question or suggestion.

How to Use

Verb stem + 는데 / Adjective stem + 은데 (for words ending in consonants) or ㄴ데 (for words ending in vowels).

Eg: 바쁜데 약속을 미뤄도 될까요? (I'm busy; should we postpone the appointment?)

Examples

i. 오늘 날씨가 좋은데 같이 산책할래요?

ii. 저는 약간 긴장되는데 괜찮을까요?

iii. 저녁 식사가 예정되어 있는데 같이 가시겠어요?

iv. 친구가 바쁜데 다른 날 만날까요?

v. 저는 준비가 됐는데 당신은요?

3. Expressing Intentions: ~기로 하다 (Deciding to Do Something)

~기로 하다 is used to express a decision or intention to do something.

How to Use

Verb stem + 기로 하다.

Eg: 만나기로 했어요 (We decided to meet).

Examples

i. 친구들과 저녁에 만나기로 했어요.

ii. 기념일을 다음 주에 축하하기로 했어요.

iii. 파티를 토요일에 열기로 했어요.

iv. 약속을 미루기로 했어요.

v. 새로운 일정을 정하기로 했어요.

IV. Exercise

1. Complete each sentence with the appropriate grammar pattern from (으)ㄹ까요?, ~는데/~은데, or ~기로 하다.

i. 우리는 이번 주에 약속을 _____ 했어요.

ii. 주말에 친구들을 _____ ?

iii.   저는 그 장소가 조금 불편한데, 다른 곳에서 _____ ?

iv.   저녁에 같이 식사 _____ ?

v. 가족과 함께 기념일을 _____ 했어요.

2. Choose the correct grammar pattern to complete each sentence appropriately.

i. 친구가 바쁜데 약속을 다음 주로 _____ ?

a) 초대할까요

b) 미루기로 했어요

c) 미룰까요

ii. 저는 오늘 준비가 안 됐는데, 내일 _____ ?

a) 할까요

b) 하기로 했어요

c) 초대할까요

iii. 가족들과 기념일을 주말에 _____ 했어요.

a) 만날까요

b) 정하기로

c) 축하하기로

iv. 이번 주말에 같이 산책 _____ ?

a) 하기로 했어요

b) 할까요

c) 하는데

v. 친구들과 저녁 식사를 _____ 했어요.

a) 초대할까요

b) 만날까요

c) 하기로

3. Transform each sentence as instructed, using the grammar patterns introduced in the chapter.

i. **Original:** 저는 친구를 초대했어요.

Change to: Ask if you should invite a friend using (으)ㄹ까요?

Answer: _____

ii. **Original:** 우리는 약속을 다음 달에 정하기로 했어요.

Change to: Ask if you should schedule the appointment for this week instead.

Answer: _____

iii. Original: 저는 준비가 됐어요.

Change to: Use ~는데 to suggest that you're ready and ask if the other person is too.

Answer: _____

iv. Original: 생일 파티를 다음 주에 열기로 했어요.

Change to: Use (으)ㄹ까요? to ask if you should have the party this week instead.

Answer: _____

v. Original: 친구들과 기념일을 축하하기로 했어요.

Change to: Use (으)ㄹ까요? to ask if you should celebrate the anniversary with friends.

Answer: _____

4. Matching Exercise with Invitations and Responses

Column A	Column B
i. 이번 주말에 같이 영화 볼까요?	a) 네, 다음 주에 파티하면 좋겠어요.
ii. 생일 파티를 다음 주에 열기로 했어요.	b) 네, 이번 주말에 영화 보러 갈게요.
iii. 새로운 약속을 정할까요?	c) 네, 모두 도착했어요.
iv. 친구가 바쁜데, 모임을 미룰까요?	d) 그럼 다음 주로 미룹시다.
v. 저는 준비가 됐는데, 다들 오셨나요?	e) 네, 새로 약속을 정해요.

Chapter- 23

I. Vocabulary

금지	prohibition
흡연	smoking
음주	drinking alcohol
소란	noise
사진촬영	photography
쓰레기	trash
음식물	food waste
휴대폰	cell phone
주차	parking
출입	entry/access
지각	lateness
무단 횡단	jaywalking
과속	speeding
표지판	sign
경고	warning
벌금	fine
위반	violation
규칙	rule
질서	order
안전	safety
신호등	traffic light
도난	theft

위험	danger
조용한	quiet
거짓말	lie
불법	illegal
부주의	carelessness
책임	responsibility
사고	accident
행동	behavior
비상구	emergency exit
주의	caution

Expressions

여기서 하면 안 돼요	You shouldn't do that here
사진을 찍으면 안 돼요	You must not take photos
음식을 먹으면 안 돼요	No eating allowed
휴대폰 사용 금지입니다	No cell phone use
출입 금지 구역(이에요]	Restricted area
여기서 뛰면 안 돼요)	Don't run here
쓰레기를 버리면 안 돼요	Do not throw trash
금연 구역(입니다)	No smoking area
속도를 줄이세요	Reduce your speed
조용히 해 주세요	Please be quiet
다른 사람에게 피해를 주지 마세요	Don't inconvenience others
무단 횡단하지 마세요	No jaywalking
이곳은 위험합니다	This area is dangerous

II. Conversation

A: 여기서는 휴대폰을 사용하면 안 돼요.

B: 아, 그래요? 왜요?

A: 조용한 공간이니까 다른 사람들을 방해하면 안 돼요.

B: 알겠어요. 그럼, 여기서 쓰레기를 버려도 되나요?

A: 네, 쓰레기는 지정된 장소에 버려야 해요.

You must not use a cell phone here.

Oh, really? Why?

It's a quiet area, so you shouldn't disturb others.

I understand. Then, can I throw trash here?

No, trash must be disposed of in designated areas.

III. Grammar

1. Expressing Prohibition: (으)면 안 된다 (Shouldn't / Mustn't)

(으)면 안 된다 is used to indicate that something is prohibited or not allowed.

How to Use

Verb stem + (으)면 안 된다

Eg: 뛰면 안 돼요 (You must not run)

Examples

i. 여기에 쓰레기를 버리면 안 돼요.

ii. 도서관에서 소리 내면 안 돼요.

iii.   음식물은 반입하면 안 돼요.

iv.   이곳에서 담배를 피우면 안 돼요.

v. 이 구역에 들어가면 안 돼요.

2. Giving Reasons: ~(으)니까 (Because/Since)

~(으)니까 is used to explain the reason or cause of something, often followed by a prohibition or caution.

How to Use

Verb/Adjective stem + ~(으)니까

Eg: 위험하니까 가까이 가지 마세요 (It's dangerous, so don't go near)

Examples

i. 도서관이니까 조용히 해야 해요.

ii. 위험하니까 물건을 만지면 안 돼요.

iii.   금연 구역이니까 담배를 피우면 안 돼요.

iv.   다른 사람들이 있으니까 소리를 내지 마세요.

v. 여기에서는 음식을 먹으면 안 되니까 주의하세요.

3. Expressing Necessity or Instructions: ~아야/어야 하다

~아야/어야 하다 is used to express that something must be done or needs to be done, often in relation to following rules or safety instructions.

How to Use

Verb stem + ~아야/어야 하다

Eg: 주의해야 해요 (You have to be cautious)

Examples

i. 교통 신호를 지켜야 해요.

ii. 안전을 위해 속도를 줄여야 해요.

iii.   이 구역에서는 주의를 기울여야 해요.

iv. 여기에서는 조용히 해야 해요.

v. 안전 장비를 착용해야 해요.

IV. Exercise

1. Fill in the Blanks with the Correct Grammar Pattern

i. 도서관에서는 소리를 내면 _____.

ii. 위험 _____ 보호 장비를 착용해야 해요.

iii. 이 구역은 금지 구역이니까 _____ 안 돼요.

iv. 주차 구역이 아니니까 여기에 주차 _____.

v. 횡단보도에서만 길을 건너야 _____.

2. Sentence Completion (Using Prohibitions and Instructions)

i. (으)면 안 된다: 여기에서는 _____ (담배를 피우다).

Answer: _____

ii. ~(으)니까: 이곳은 위험 _____ (조심하다).

Answer: _____

iii. ~아야/어야 하다: 쓰레기는 _____ (지정된 장소에 버리다).

Answer: _____

iv. (으)면 안 된다: 박물관에서 _____ (소리를 내다).

Answer: _____

3. Match each statement in Column A with the correct prohibition or instruction in Column B.

Column A	Column B
i. 도서관이니까	a) 피우면 안 돼요
ii. 위험하니까	b) 조용히 해야 해요
iii. 이곳에서 담배를	c) 가까이 가지 마세요
iv. 음식물을	d) 가지고 들어오면 안 돼요
v. 조용한 구역이니까	e) 소리 내면 안 돼요

4. Translate each sentence into Korean using (으)면 안 된다 for prohibited actions.

i. You must not eat food in the library.

Answer: _____

ii. It's a hospital, so you must not make noise.

Answer: _____

iii. You must not enter the restricted area.

Answer: _____

iv. You should not use your phone in the theater.

Answer: _____

v. You must not park here.

Answer: _____

Chapter- 24
SOCIAL ETIQUETTE

I. Vocabulary

연세	age (honorific)
성함	name (honorific)
말씀	words/speech (honorific)
진지	meal (honorific)
댁	house (honorific)
편찮으시다	to be ill (honorific)
주무시다	to sleep (honorific)
드시다	to eat/drink (honorific)
계시다	to be/stay (honorific)
생신	birthday (honorific)
자녀분	children (honorific)
존함	name (formal)
모시다	to serve (honorific)
여쭙다	to ask respectfully
찾아뵙다	to visit someone (honorific)
존경	respect
예절	etiquette
공손함	politeness
존댓말	formal speech
식사 예절	table manners
방문 예절	visiting etiquette
인사	greeting

배려	consideration
규칙	rules
존경심	respectfulness
지키다	to observe (rules)
상석	seat of honor
차례	order/turn
성실함	sincerity
겸손	humility
양보	yielding

Expressions

안녕히 주무세요	Please sleep well (goodnight, honorific)
식사하셨어요?	Did you have a meal?
연세가 어떻게 되세요?	What is your age? (honorific)
성함이 어떻게 되세요?	What is your name? (honorific)
말씀해 주세요	Please speak (honorific)
진지 드셨어요?	Did you have a meal? (honorific)
편찮으세요?	Are you feeling unwell? (honorific)
찾아뵙고 싶습니다	I would like to visit you
모셔 드릴게요	I will escort you (honorific)
존경하고 있습니다	I respect you
시간을 내 주셔서 감사합니다	Thank you for making time
잘 부탁드립니다	Please take care of me
예의를 지켜야 해요	You should observe proper manners

II. Conversation

A: 할머니께서 식사하셨어요?   Did grandmother have her meal?

B: 네, 식사하셨다고 하셨어요.   Yes, she said she did.

할머니께서는 지금 주무세요.   She's sleeping now.

A: 그렇군요. 제가 나중에   I see. I'll visit her later

찾아뵙고 인사드릴게요.   and greet her.

B: 네, 할머니께서도 기뻐하실   Yes, she will be happy

거예요.   to see you.

III. Grammar

1. Honorifics: (으)시~ (Honorific Verb Form)

(으)시 is added to verbs to convey respect toward the subject, commonly used when referring to someone older or in a higher position.

How to Use

Verb stem + (으)시.

Eg: 가다 (to go) → 가시다 (to go, honorific)

Examples

i. 선생님께서 학교에 가세요.

ii. 어머님께서 식사하셨어요.

iii. 할아버지께서 주무세요.

iv. 부모님께서 여행을 가셨어요.

v. 할머니께서 말씀하셨어요.

2. Expressing Obligation: ~아야/어야 되다/하다 (Must/Need to)

~아야/어야 되다/하다 is used to express obligation or necessity, meaning "must" or "need to."

How to Use
Verb stem + ~아야/어야 되다/하다

Eg: 지키다 (to observe) → 지켜야 해요 (must observe)

Examples

i. 어른께 먼저 인사해야 해요.

ii. 예의를 지켜야 합니다.

iii. 다른 사람을 배려해야 해요.

iv. 약속을 지켜야 합니다.

v. 자리를 양보해야 합니다.

3. Indirect Quotation: ~라고 하다 (To Say)

~라고 하다 is used to indirectly quote what someone said, which is often used in polite speech to relay information respectfully.

How to Use
Quotation + ~라고 하다

Eg: 시간이 없다고 하셨어요 (He/she said that they don't have time)

Examples

i. 선생님께서 내일 오신다고 하셨어요.

ii. 어머님께서 식사하셨다고 하셨어요.

iii. 친구가 늦을 거라고 했어요.

iv. 부모님이 여행 중이라고 하셨어요.

v. 할머니께서 진지를 드셨다고 하셨어요.

IV. Exercise

1. Complete each sentence with the correct honorific form using (으)시~

i. 어머님께서 지금 집에 _____ (계시다).

Answer: _____

ii. 선생님께서 학교에 _____ (가다).

Answer: _____

iii. 할아버지께서 텔레비전을 _____ (보다).

Answer: _____

iv. 부모님께서 여행을 _____ (**Past Tense** 가다).

Answer: _____

v. 할머니께서 말씀을 _____ (**Past Tense** 하다).

Answer: _____

2. Multiple Choice (Expressing Obligation ~아야/어야 되다/하다)

i. 어른께 _____ 해요. (You must greet elders.)

a) 인사해야

b) 존경해야

c) 잊어버려야

ii. 약속을 _____ 합니다. (You must keep your promise.)

a) 깨야

b) 지켜야

c) 잃어버려야

iii. 다른 사람을 _____ 해요. (You must be considerate of others.)

a) 보세요

b) 방해해야

c) 배려해야

iv. 예의를 _____ 해요. (You must follow etiquette.)

a) 지켜야

b) 깨어야

c) 없애야

v. 자리를 _____ 해야 합니다. (You need to offer your seat.)

a) 가져야

b) 양보해야

c) 버려야

3. Fill in the Blanks with Obligation (아야/어야 되다/하다)

i. 예의를 _____ 합니다. **(to observe)**

Answer: _____

ii. 다른 사람들을 _____ 해요. **(to be considerate)**

Answer: _____

iii. 약속을 _____ 합니다. **(to keep)**

Answer: _____

iv. 어른들을 _____ 해야 해요. **(to show respect)**

Answer: _____

v. 교실에서는 _____ 해야 합니다. **(to be quiet)**

Answer: _____

4. Match each standard form in Column A with the correct honorific expression in Column B.

Column A	Column B
i. 나이	a) 성함
ii. 이름	b) 연세
iii. 집	c) 편찮으시다
iv. 밥	d) 진지
v. 아프다	e) 댁

5. Translation Practice with Etiquette Expressions

i. Grandmother said to be careful.

ii. Mother said to eat well.

iii. The teacher said that he/she will see you tomorrow.

iv. I need to offer my seat to elders.

v. Father said that he is going on a business trip.

Chapter- 25
SCHOOL AND STUDIES

I. Vocabulary

공부	study
학습	learning
교육	education
과목	subject
교재/교과서	textbook
교실	classroom
수업	class
강의	lecture
과제	assignment
시험	exam
복습	review
예습	preview
질문	question
답변	answer
성적	grade
노트	note
책상	desk
교사	teacher
교수	professor
학생	student
교장	principal
장학금	scholarship

연구	research
조사	survey
성공	success
실패	failure
졸업	graduation
입학	entrance/admission
지식	knowledge
능력	ability
목표	goal
성과	achievement
숙제	homework
학기	semester
문제	problem/question
방법	method

Expressions

질문 있어요?	Do you have a question?
답변해 주세요	Please give an answer
오늘의 과제는 무엇인가요?	What is today's assignment?
성적이 어때요?	How are your grades?
시험 준비 잘 하세요	Prepare well for the exam
시험에 합격했어요	I passed the exam
복습이 중요해요	Review is important
열심히 공부하세요	Study hard

II. Conversation

A: 이번 시험은 준비하기 어려운 것 같아요.

I think it's hard to prepare for this exam.

B: 맞아요. 그래서 좋은 성적을 받기 위해서 매일 복습하고 있어요.

I agree. That's why I review every day to get good grades.

A: 저도요. 공부하면서 음악을 듣기도 해요.

Me too. I also listen to music while studying.

B: 네, 도움이 되죠. 저희 모두 좋은 결과가 나오길 바라요.

Yes, it helps. I hope we get good results.

III. Grammar

1. Expressing Simultaneous Actions: (으)면서 (While/As)

(으)면서 is used to indicate two actions happening simultaneously, meaning "while" or "as".

How to Use
Verb stem + (으)면서

Eg: 공부하면서 음악을 들어요 (I listen to music while studying).

Examples

i. 노트를 정리하면서 강의를 들어요.

ii. 교과서를 읽으면서 복습해요.

iii. 문제를 풀면서 질문을 해요.

iv. 공부하면서 간식을 먹어요.

v. 숙제를 하면서 예습도 해요.

2. Expressing Ease or Difficulty: -기 쉽다/어렵다

-기 쉽다 is used to indicate that something is easy to do, while -기 어렵다 is used to indicate that something is difficult to do.

How to Use
Verb stem + -기 쉽다/어렵다

Eg: 문제를 이해하기 어려워요 (It's difficult to understand the problem).

Examples
i. 이 과목은 공부하기 쉬워요.

ii. 시험 준비하기 어렵네요.

iii. 문제를 푸는 것이 쉽지 않아요.

iv. 장학금은 받기 어렵지만 불가능한 것은 아니에요.

v. 이 교재는 읽기 쉬워서 좋아요.

3. Expressing Purpose: -기 위해서 (In Order to)

-기 위해서 is used to express purpose or intent, meaning "in order to" or "for the purpose of".

How to Use
Verb stem + -기 위해서

Eg: 좋은 성적을 받기 위해서 열심히 공부해요

(I study hard in order to get good grades).

Examples
i. 장학금을 받기 위해서 열심히 공부해요.

ii. 시험에 합격하기 위해서 준비해요.

iii. 좋은 성적을 얻기 위해 복습을 해요.

iv. 목표를 이루기 위해 노력해요.

v. 지식을 넓히기 위해 많은 책을 읽어요.

IV. Exercise

1. Fill in the Blanks with (으)면서 (While/As)

i. 저는 시험 준비를 _____ 친구와 이야기를 해요. (하다)

Answer: _____

ii. 수업을 _____ 노트를 정리해요. (듣다)

Answer: _____

iii. 문제를 _____ 질문을 해요. (풀다)

Answer: _____

iv. 교과서를 _____ 복습을 해요. (읽다)

Answer: _____

v. 저는 도서관에서 공부를 _____ 음악을 들어요. (하다)

Answer: _____

2. Multiple Choice (Using -기 쉽다/어렵다 for Ease or Difficulty)

i. 이 교과서는 _____ (easy to read).

a) 읽기 쉬워요

b) 읽기 어려워요

c) 읽기 쉽지 않아요

ii. 시험 문제는 _____ (difficult to solve).

a) 풀기 쉬워요

b) 풀기 어려워요

c) 풀기 가능해요

iii. 영어 단어를 매일 공부하면 _____ (easy to remember).

a) 외우기 어려워요

b) 외우기 쉬워요

c) 외우기 필요해요

iv. 이 과제는 _____ (challenging to complete).

a) 완성하기 쉬워요

b) 완성하기 어려워요

c) 완성하기 편해요

v. 교과서가 복잡해서 _____ (difficult to understand).

a) 이해하기 쉬워요

b) 이해하기 어려워요

c) 이해하기 필요해요

3. Translation Practice with Purpose (-기 위해서)

i. I study hard to pass the exam.

Answer: _____

ii. She reads books to gain more knowledge.

Answer: _____

iii. They practice every day to improve their skills.

Answer: _____

iv. I do my homework in order to get a good grade.

Answer: _____

v. He asks questions to understand the lesson better.

Answer: _____

4. Match each study-related activity in Column A with the appropriate explanation in Column B.

Column A	Column B
i. 수업을 들으면서	a) 교재를 복습해요
ii. 시험을 준비하기 위해서	b) 쉽게 이해할 수 있어요
iii. 공부하면서	c) 선생님의 설명을 듣고 있어요
iv. 예습을 하면	d) 열심히 공부해야 해요
v. 장학금을 받기 위해서	e) 선생님께 물어볼 수 있어요

5. Rearrange the words in each sentence to create a grammatically correct sentence

i. 공부를 / 들어요 / 저는 / 하면서 / 음악을

Answer: _____

ii. 복습을 / 해요 / 교과서를 / 읽으면서

Answer: _____

iii. 필기를 / 정리해요 / 강의를 / 들으면서

Answer: _____

iv. 문제를 / 친구와 / 질문을 / 풀면서 / 해요

Answer: _____

v. 저는 / 들으면서 / 노트를 / 정리해요 / 수업을

Answer: _____

Chapter- 26

HEALTH AND WELLNESS

I. Vocabulary

머리	head
얼굴	face
눈	eye
코	nose
입	mouth
귀	ear
목	neck/throat
어깨	shoulder
팔	arm
손	hand
손목	wrist
발	foot
다리	leg
무릎	knee
허리	waist
가슴	chest
배	stomach
등	back
손가락	finger
발가락	toe

두통	headache
열	fever
기침	cough
콧물	runny nose
목 아픔	sore throat
복통	stomachache
어지러움	dizziness
근육통	muscle pain
피곤함	fatigue
소화 불량	indigestion
몸살	body aches
열이 나다	have a fever
배가 아프다	stomach hurts
토하다	to vomit
재채기	sneeze
눈이 아픔	eye pain
가래	phlegm
땀이 나다	to sweat
무기력	lethargy

Expressions

어디가 아프세요?	Where does it hurt?
열이 있어요?	Do you have a fever?
기침이 나요	I have a cough
의사와 상담해야 해요	You should consult a doctor

약을 드세요	Take your medicine
진료를 받으세요	Get a check-up
차가운 음식을 먹지 마세요	Don't eat cold food
안정을 취하세요	Take a rest
몸이 안 좋네요	You look unwell
너무 무리하지 마세요	Don't overdo it
물을 많이 드세요	Drink plenty of water
규칙적인 식사를 하세요	Eat regular meals
스트레스를 피하세요	Avoid stress

II. Conversation

A: 어디가 아프세요?

Where does it hurt?

B: 머리가 아프고 열이 나요.

I have a headache and a fever.

A: 열이 있으면 병원에 가는 게 좋아요. 약을 먹은 후에 푹 쉬세요.

If you have fever, it's better to go to the clinic. Rest well after taking medicine.

B: 네, 알겠습니다. 차가운 음식을 먹지 않을게요. 감사합니다.

Yes, I understand. I won't eat cold food. Thank you.

III. Grammar

1. Describing Actions After an Event: -(으)ㄴ 후에 (After)

-(으)ㄴ 후에 is used to describe an action that happens after something else. The form varies based on whether a noun, verb, or time expression is being used.

How to Use

- **Verb stem + -(으)ㄴ 후에**

Eg: 식사한 후에 약을 드세요 (Take the medicine after a meal)

- **Noun + 후에**

Eg: 치료 후에 푹 쉬세요 (Get plenty of rest after treatment)

- **Time Expression + 후에**

Eg: 한 시간 후에 돌아오세요 (Come back after an hour)

Examples

i. 진찰을 받은 후에 약을 드세요.

ii. 운동한 후에 스트레칭을 하세요.

iii. 수술 후에 조심하세요.

iv. 두통이 나아진 후에 출근하세요.

v. 약을 먹은 후에 물을 많이 마시세요.

2. Polite Prohibition: -지 마세요 (Please Don't)

-지 마세요 is used to politely ask someone not to do something.

How to Use

Verb stem + -지 마세요

Eg: 너무 무리하지 마세요 (Don't overdo it)

Examples

i. 차가운 음식을 먹지 마세요.

ii. 무리하지 마세요.

iii. 몸이 안 좋으면 운동하지 마세요.

iv. 소리를 지르지 마세요.

v. 짠 음식을 많이 먹지 마세요.

3. Suggesting an Action for Relief: -는 게 좋다 (It's Better to)

-는 게 좋다 is used to make a suggestion or give advice, often in the context of health or well-being.

How to Use

Verb stem + -는 게 좋다

Eg: 쉬는 게 좋다 (It's better to rest)

Examples

i. 열이 있으면 병원에 가는 게 좋아요.

ii. 피곤할 때는 쉬는 게 좋아요.

iii. 기침이 날 때는 따뜻한 차를 마시는 게 좋아요.

iv. 무리하지 말고 편안하게 쉬는 게 좋습니다.

v. 두통이 있으면 조용한 곳에서 쉬는 게 좋아요.

IV. Exercise

1. Fill in the Blanks with -(으)ㄴ 후에 (After)

i. 식사 _____ 약을 드세요.

ii. 진료를 받은 _____ 집에 가세요.

iii. 운동 _____ 물을 많이 마시세요.

iv. 약을 먹은 _____ 푹 쉬세요.

v. 잠을 잔 _____ 기분이 나아질 거예요.

2. Fill in the Blanks with -지 마세요 (Don't)

i. 열이 있을 때는 무리하지 _____.

Answer: _____

ii. 목이 아플 때는 차가운 음료를 마시지 _____.

Answer: _____

iii. 배가 아플 때는 기름진 음식을 먹지 _____.

Answer: _____

iv. 감기에 걸렸을 때는 찬바람을 쐬지 _____.

Answer: _____

v. 두통이 있을 때는 소리를 지르지 _____.

Answer: _____

3. Complete each sentence using -는 게 좋다 to give advice.

i. 두통이 있으면 조용한 곳에서 _____. (It's better to rest)

Answer: _____

ii. 감기에 걸렸을 때는 따뜻한 차를 _____. (It's better to drink)

Answer: _____

iii. 피곤할 때는 일찍 _____. (It's better to sleep)

Answer: _____

iv. 몸이 안 좋으면 집에서 _____. (It's better to stay)

Answer: _____

v. 열이 있을 때는 병원에 _____. (It's better to go)

Answer: _____

4. Match Column A with the Column B.

Column A	Column B
i. 두통이 있을 때	a) 따뜻한 차를 마시는 게 좋아요
ii. 열이 높을 때	b) 푹 쉬는 게 좋아요
iii. 목이 아플 때	c) 병원에 가는 게 좋아요
iv. 피곤할 때	d) 조용한 곳에서 쉬세요
v. 배가 아플 때	e) 찬 음식을 먹지 마세요

5. Complete the Sentences with given vocabulary and grammar.

Vocabulary	Grammar
머리 ,약	-(으)ㄴ 후에
기침 ,목	-지 마세요
두통, 식사	-는 게 좋다

i. _____이 아프면 조용한 곳에서 쉬는 _____.

ii. 피곤할 때는 푹 쉬고 물을 많이 마시는 _____.

iii. 감기에 걸렸을 때는 따뜻한 차를 마시는 _____.

iv. 진료를 받은 _____ 집에서 푹 쉬세요.

v. _____이 나면 병원에 가는 게 좋습니다.

vi. _____이 있으면 찬 음료를 마시지 _____.

vii. ___를 한 ___ 약을 드세요.

viii. _____가 아프면 차가운 음식을 먹지 _____.

Chapter- 27
NAVIGATING DIRECTIONS

I. Vocabulary

왼쪽	left
오른쪽	right
앞	front
뒤	back
위	top/above
아래	below/under
안	inside
밖	outside
건너편	across from
맞은편	opposite side
옆	next to
가까이	nearby
멀리	far
모퉁이/코너	corner
횡단보도	crosswalk
교차로	intersection
신호등	traffic light
지하	basement
층	floor
엘리베이터	elevator
계단	stairs
입구	entrance

출구	exit
길	street
건물	building
방향	direction
사거리	four-way intersection
길가	roadside
도보	on foot

Expressions

어디로 가야 해요?	Where should I go?
이 근처에 있어요?	Is it nearby?
몇 층에 있어요?	Which floor is it on?
길을 알려 주세요	Please show me the way
엘리베이터를 타세요	Take the elevator
계단으로 올라가세요	Go up the stairs
여기에서 가까운가요?	Is it close from here?
얼마나 멀어요?	How far is it?
오른쪽으로 돌아가세요	Turn right
횡단보도를 건너세요	Cross the crosswalk
이 길을 따라가세요	Follow this road
출구는 어디에 있어요?	Where is the exit?
지하 1층에 있습니다	It's on basement level 1

II. Conversation

A: 혹시 여기서 엘리베이터가 어디에 있습니까?

Do you know where the elevator is from here?

B: 엘리베이터는 저쪽 왼쪽에 있습니다. 몇 층에 가실 겁니까?

The elevator is to the left over there. Which floor are you going to?

A: 3층에 있는 도서관에 가려고 합니다.

I'm going to the library on the 3rd floor.

B: 그럼 3층에 도착한 후에 오른쪽으로 가세요. 도서관이 보일 거예요.

Then, after you reach the 3rd floor, go right. You'll see the library.

A: 네, 감사합니다.

Thank you.

III. Grammar

1. Conditionals with -면 (If) using 혹시 and 만일

-면 is used to form conditional sentences, meaning "if." Adding 혹시 or 만일 makes the sentence more polite or adds a sense of possibility.

How to Use

- **Verb/Adjective + -면**
- 혹시 **or** 만일 **can be added at the beginning for emphasis.**

Eg: 혹시 오른쪽으로 가면 출구가 있어요?

   (If you go right, is there an exit?)

Examples

i. 혹시 왼쪽으로 가면 계단이 있나요?

ii. 만일 지하에 있으면 어떻게 가야 해요?

iii. 이 길을 따라가면 교차로가 나와요.

iv. 혹시 신호등이 보이면 거기서 왼쪽으로 가세요.

v. 혹시 출구를 찾으면 저에게 알려 주세요.

2. Polite Inquiry and Statements: ㅂ/습니까? and -ㅂ/습니다

ㅂ/습니까? is used to form polite questions, while -ㅂ/습니다 is used for polite statements, often in directions or formal situations.

How to Use

- **Verb stem + ㅂ/습니까? for questions**
- **Verb stem + -ㅂ/습니다 for statements**

Eg: 여기에서 왼쪽으로 가면 엘리베이터가 있습니까?

(If you go left from here, is there an elevator?)

Examples

i. 3층에 병원이 있습니까?

ii. 계단은 저쪽에 있습니다.

iii. 2층으로 올라가면 입구가 보입니까?

iv. 오른쪽으로 가면 출구가 있습니다.

v. 이 건물에 화장실이 있습니까?

3. Expressing Location and Existence with -에 있다/없다 (To Be/Not to Be at a Location)

ㅂ/습니까? is used to form polite questions, while -ㅂ/습니다 is used for polite statements, often in directions or formal situations.

How to Use

• **Noun + -**에 있다/없다

Eg: 엘리베이터는 지하 1층에 있어요.

　　(The elevator is on basement level 1.)

Examples

i. 도서관은 2층에 있어요.

ii. 출구는 이쪽에 없습니다.

iii.　엘리베이터는 오른쪽에 있습니다.

iv.　1층에 안내 데스크가 있어요.

v. 화장실은 복도 끝에 있어요.

IV. Exercise

1. Match the Directions and Responses

Column A	Column B
i. 혹시 엘리베이터가 어디에 있습니까?	a) 네, 2층에 약국이 있습니다.
ii. 이 길을 따라가면 무엇이 있습니까?	b) 계단 대신 엘리베이터를 타세요.
iii. 만일 계단이 없다면 어떻게 해야 해요?	c) 엘리베이터는 입구 옆에 있습니다.
iv. 2층에 약국이 있습니까?	d) 첫 번째 모퉁이에서 오른쪽으로 가세요.
v. 3층에 도착한 후에 어디로 가야 합니까?	e) 교차로가 나옵니다.

2. Fill in the Blanks with the Correct Grammar Pattern

i. 혹시 출구를 찾으면 저에게 _____.

Answer: _____

ii. 1층에 약국이 _____?

Answer: _____

iii. 엘리베이터는 2층에 _____.

Answer: _____

iv. 이 길을 따라가면 교차로가 _____.

Answer: _____

v. 이 건물에 주차장이 _____?

Answer: _____

3. Translation Practice Using Grammar and Vocabulary

i. If you go to the 2nd floor, is there a restroom?

Answer: _____

ii. Please tell me where the exit is.

Answer: _____

iii. Is there a pharmacy on the 1st floor?

Answer: _____

iv. The elevator is near the entrance.

Answer: _____

v. After you reach the 3rd floor, turn left.

Answer: _____

4. Choose the correct vocabulary word to complete each sentence.

i. 왼쪽에 있는 _____을(를) 지나가세요.

a) 입구

b) 교차로

c) 엘리베이터

ii. 이 길을 따라가면 _____가 나옵니다.

a) 사거리

b) 계단

c) 지하

iii. 도서관은 길 ___에 있습니다.

a) 맞은편에

b) 옆에

c) 건너편

iv. 건물의 _____에서 엘리베이터를 찾으세요.

a) 길가

b) 입구

c) 교차로

v. _____에서 오른쪽으로 돌면 화장실이 있습니다.

a) 계단

b) 코너

c) 길

5. Use the options below to complete each sentence based on the given scenario.

Options

왼쪽에 있어요, 오른쪽으로 도세요, 건너편에 있어요

계단을 내려가세요, 옆에 있어요

Questions:

i. **"Excuse me, where is the bank?"**

Context: The bank is directly across from where you are standing.

Answer: _____

ii. **"Where is the exit to the building?"**

Context: After walking straight ahead, you'll need to turn right to find the exit.

Answer: _____

iii. "I took the elevator to the 2nd floor. Now, where should I go to find the restroom?"

Context: After reaching the 2nd floor, the restroom is on your left.

Answer: _____

iv. "I need to find the library on the 1st floor. How do I get there?"

Context: The library entrance is at the bottom of the stairs on the 1st floor.

Answer: _____

v. "Where can I find the pharmacy in this building?"

Context: The pharmacy is located right next to the information desk.

Answer: _____

Chapter- 28
BANKING AND FINANCE

I. Vocabulary

계좌	account
통장	bankbook
은행	bank
ATM	ATM
카드	card
비밀번호	password
입금	deposit
출금	withdrawal
송금	transfer
환전	currency exchange
잔액	balance
수수료	fee
이자	interest
직원	staff
번호표	number ticket
신분증	ID card
도장	seal/stamp
체크카드	debit card
현금	cash
통장정리	bankbook update

자동이체	automatic transfer/ payments
현금인출기	ATM machine
인터넷뱅킹	internet banking
영업시간	business hours
대기시간	waiting time

Expressions

계좌를 만들려고 해요	I want to open an account
현금을 입금하고 싶어요	I'd like to deposit cash
잔액이 얼마인가요?	What is the balance?
비밀번호를 입력해 주세요	Please enter your password
수수료가 얼마예요?	How much is the fee?
이자율이 어떻게 되나요?	What is the interest rate?
번호표를 뽑아 주세요	Please take a number ticket
도장이 필요해요	I need a seal/stamp
대기 시간이 얼마나 돼요?	How long is the waiting time?
송금을 할 수 있나요?	Can I make a transfer?
체크카드를 발급해 주세요	Please issue a debit card
ATM에서 출금하려고 해요	I want to withdraw money from the ATM
현금인출기 어디에 있어요?	Where is the ATM?
통장 정리를 해야 해요	I need to update my bankbook

II. Conversation

A: 안녕하세요. 계좌를 만들려고 하는데요.

Hello. I'd like to open an account.

B: 안녕하세요. 신분증을 가져오셨나요?

Hello. Did you bring your ID?

A: 네, 여기 있습니다.

Yes, here it is.

B: 그럼, 번호표를 뽑으시면 돼요. 번호가 불리면 도장도 필요합니다.

Then, just take a number ticket. When your number is called, you'll also need a stamp.

A: 네, 감사합니다.

Okay, thank you.

III. Grammar

1. Expressing Intention: -(으)려고 (To Intend to)

-(으)려고 is used to express the speaker's intention to do something or a planned action, meaning "to do" or "in order to do."

How to Use
Verb stem + -(으)려고

Eg: 계좌를 만들려고 해요 (I intend to open an account)

Examples

i. 체크카드를 발급받으려고 은행에 갔어요.

ii. 출금하려고 ATM을 찾고 있어요.

iii. 통장을 정리하려고 은행에 방문했어요.

iv. 송금을 하려고 직원에게 문의했어요.

v. 계좌를 확인하려고 비밀번호를 입력했어요.

2. Simple Conditions with -(으)면 되다

-(으)면 되다 is used to state that something can be done under certain conditions or if a certain action is taken, meaning "If you do ___, it's okay."

How to Use

Verb stem + -(으)면 되다

Eg: 비밀번호를 입력하면 돼요 (You just need to enter your password)

Examples

i. 신분증을 가져오면 돼요.

ii. 통장을 제출하면 계좌 확인이 돼요.

iii. ATM에서 송금하면 돼요.

iv. 비밀번호를 입력하면 출금이 가능해요.

v. 번호표를 뽑으면 직원이 부를 거예요.

3. Polite Requests and Commands: -아/어 주세요 (Please Do)

-아/어 주세요 is used to politely ask someone to do something for you, such as making a request or asking for assistance.

How to Use

Verb stem + -아/어 주세요

Eg: 도장을 찍어 주세요 (Please stamp it for me)

Examples

i. 현금을 입금해 주세요.

ii. 통장 정리를 해 주세요.

iii. 체크카드를 발급해 주세요.

iv. 계좌를 확인해 주세요.

IV. Exercise

1. Based on each scenario, select the most appropriate action from the options provided.

Options:
- 번호표를 뽑으세요
- 통장을 정리해 주세요
- 잔액을 확인해 주세요
- 체크카드를 발급해 주세요
- 비밀번호를 입력하세요

i. You want to know how much money is in your account.
Answer: _____

ii. You are at the bank and need to wait for your turn.
Answer: _____

iii. You would like to get a debit card for your account.
Answer: _____

iv. The staff member asks you to confirm your identity at the ATM.
Answer: _____

v. You want to make sure your bankbook is up to date.
Answer: _____

2. Choosing the Correct Polite Request with -아/어 주세요

i. You want to update your bankbook.

a) 통장을 정리해 주세요

b) 계좌를 확인해 주세요

c) 송금을 해 주세요

ii. You need assistance with currency exchange.

a) 비밀번호를 입력해 주세요

b) 환전을 도와주세요

c) 현금을 입금해 주세요

iii.. You want to check your balance.

a) 송금을 도와주세요

b) 잔액을 확인해 주세요

c) 통장을 만들어 주세요

iv. You need a new debit card.

a) 체크카드를 발급해 주세요

b) 통장 정리를 해 주세요

c) 수수료를 계산해 주세요

v. You want the teller to deposit cash for you.

a) 계좌를 열어 주세요

b) 현금을 입금해 주세요

c) 계좌를 정리해 주세요

3. Translate each sentence into Korean using -(으)면 되다.

i. Just take a number ticket and wait.

ii. If you enter your PIN, you can withdraw money.

iii. If you have your ID, you can open an account.

iv. You just need to press the keypad.

v. If you submit your bankbook, you can check the balance.

4. Match each question in Column A with the most appropriate response in Column B.

<table>
<tr><td>**Column A**</td><td>**Column B**</td></tr>
<tr><td>i. 이 계좌의 잔액이 얼마입니까?</td><td>a) 직원에게 문의해 주세요.</td></tr>
<tr><td>ii. 계좌를 만들려면 무엇이 필요합니까?</td><td>b) 신분증이 필요합니다.</td></tr>
<tr><td>iii. 송금하려면 어디로 가야 합니까?</td><td>c) 잔액을 확인해 드릴게요.</td></tr>
<tr><td>iv. 수수료는 얼마입니까?</td><td>d) 은행에 직접 오셔야 합니다.</td></tr>
<tr><td>v. 통장을 잃어버리면 어떻게 해야 합니까?</td><td>e) 수수료는 송금 금액에 따라 달라집니다.</td></tr>
</table>

Chapter- 29
MAIL AND DELIVERY

I. Vocabulary

소포	package
우편	mail
우체국	post office
우편물	mail (item)
우편함	mailbox
우편번호	postal code
택배	courier
배송	delivery
발송	shipment
수신인	recipient
보내다	to send
받다	to receive
주소	address
송장	invoice
배달	delivery
수령	pickup
반송	return
발송비/배송비	shipping fee
포장	packing
특급	express
등기	registered mail
봉투	envelope

요금	fee
분실	loss
운송장	waybill
서명	signature
배송 조회	delivery tracking

Expressions

우편물을 보내려고 해요	I want to send a mail item
소포를 받고 싶어요	I'd like to receive a package
수신인 이름을 적어 주세요	Please write the recipient's name
배송비는 얼마인가요?	How much is the delivery fee?
특급 배송으로 보내 주세요	Please send it via express delivery
주소를 정확히 써 주세요	Please write the address accurately
포장해 주세요	Please pack it
언제 도착할까요?	When will it arrive?
서명해 주세요	Please sign here
분실되면 어떻게 해야 하나요?	What should I do if it's lost?
반송이 가능한가요?	Is it possible to return it?
우체국은 어디에 있어요?	Where is the post office?
송장 번호를 알려 주세요	Please tell me the tracking number

II. Conversation

A: 안녕하세요, 소포를 보내려고 합니다.

Hello, I'd like to send a package.

B: 네, 수신인 이름과 주소를 적어 주십시오.

Sure, please write the recipient's name and address.

A: 네, 그리고 특급으로 보내 주세요.

Okay, and please send it by express delivery.

B: 알겠습니다. 배송비는 5,000원입니다. 요금을 지불해 주십시오.

Got it. The delivery fee is 5,000 won. Please pay here.

A: 여기 있습니다. 언제 도착할까요?

Here you go. When will it arrive?

B: 내일 도착할 예정입니다. 감사합니다.

It should arrive tomorrow. Thank you.

III. Grammar

1. Expressing Direction or Means: -(으)로 (By/With/To)

-(으)로 is used to indicate direction, a means, or a method, meaning "by," "with," or "to."

How to Use

Noun + -(으)로

Eg: 우체국으로 가세요 (Go to the post office)

Examples

i. 우체국으로 가서 소포를 보내세요.

ii. 이 소포를 등기로 보내 주세요.

iii. 우편번호를 사용해서 주소를 입력하세요.

iv. 택배로 배송할 수 있나요?

v. 이 소포를 특급으로 보내고 싶어요.

2. Polite Requests or Commands: -(으)십시오

-(으)십시오 is a polite command form, often used in formal settings like postal services to request or instruct someone to do something.

How to Use

Verb stem + -(으)십시오

Eg: 주소를 확인하십시오 (Please check the address)

Examples

i. 서명해 주십시오.

ii. 주소를 정확히 써 주십시오.

iii. 송장 번호를 확인하십시오.

iv. 요금을 지불하십시오.

v. 우편번호를 적으십시오.

3. Expressing Necessity or Requirement: -아/어야 하다

-아/어야 하다 is used to express that something must or needs to be done.

How to Use

Verb stem + -아/어야 하다

Eg: 수신인 이름을 적어야 해요 (You need to write the recipient's name)

Examples

i. 주소를 정확히 적어야 해요.

ii. 요금을 지불해야 합니다.

iii. 송장 번호를 확인해야 해요.

iv. 소포를 받으려면 신분증이 있어야 해요.

v. 반송하려면 원래 포장이 있어야 해요.

IV. Exercise

1. Fill in each blank with the correct word or grammar pattern from the vocabulary options provided.

송장 (waybill), 요금 (fee), 특급 (express), 우체국 (post office),
서명 (signature)

i. 소포를 보내기 전에 _____을 지불해야 합니다.

ii. 이 소포를 _____으로 보내 주세요. 빨리 도착해야 해요.

iii. 소포를 찾으려면 _____ 번호를 확인하세요.

iv. 반드시 _____을 해야 소포를 수령할 수 있습니다.

v. 소포를 보내려면 _____에 가서 접수해 주세요

2. Choose the Correct Form with -(으)십시오

i. You need the customer to write the recipient's name.

a) 수신인 이름을 적어 주십시오

b) 송장 번호를 확인하십시오

c) 요금을 확인하십시오

ii. The address needs to be written clearly.

a) 서명해 주십시오

b) 주소를 써 주십시오

c) 주소를 정확히 적어 주십시오

iii. The customer needs to check the tracking number.

a) 요금을 찍으십시오

b) 송장 번호를 확인하십시오

c) 수신인 이름을 찍으십시오

iv. The customer should pay the delivery fee.

a) 요금을 지불하십시오

b) 송금을 하십시오

c) 수령을 하십시오

v. The document should be placed in the envelope.

a) 송장을 넣으십시오

b) 봉투에 넣으십시오

c) 포장을 하십시오

3. Translate each sentence into Korean using -아/어야 하다.

i. You need to write the recipient's address accurately.

Answer: _____

ii. You must bring an ID to pick up the package.

Answer: _____

iii. You need to pay the shipping fee.

Answer: _____

iv.. The package must be packed securely.

Answer: _____

v. You must check the tracking number to find the status.

Answer: _____

4. Match each situation in Column A with the most appropriate instruction in Column B.

Column A	Column B
i. 송장을 분실했을 때	a) 요금을 지불하십시오
ii. 배송비가 있을 때	b) 직원에게 문의하십시오
iii. 서류를 안전하게 보내고 싶을 때	c) 등기 우편으로 보내십시오
	d) 송장을 다시 요청하십시오
iv. 소포를 빠르게 보내고 싶을 때	e) 특급으로 발송해 주세요
v. 반송이 가능한지 알고 싶을 때	

Chapter- 30
TALKING ABOUT THE WEATHER

I. Vocabulary

날씨	weather
맑음	clear
흐림	cloudy
비	rain
눈	snow
바람	wind
태양	sun
폭우	heavy rain
태풍	typhoon
소나기	shower
구름	cloud
안개	fog
습도	humidity
번개	lightning
천둥	thunder
기온	temperature
더위	heat
추위	cold
온도	temperature
습하다	humid
건조하다	dry
쌀쌀하다	chilly

무덥다	muggy
화창하다	sunny
시원하다	cool
따뜻하다	warm
춥다	cold
덥다	hot

Expressions

오늘 날씨가 어때요?	How is the weather today?
기온이 얼마나 돼요?	What's the temperature?
바람이 많이 불어요	It's very windy
눈이 올 것 같아요	It looks like it will snow
비가 내릴 것 같아요	It looks like it will rain
오늘은 맑아요	Today is clear
습도가 높아요	It's humid
천둥이 쳐요	There's thunder
날씨가 너무 춥네요	The weather is so cold
주말에 비가 올까요?	Will it rain on the weekend?
화창한 날씨네요	It's sunny weather
밖에 나갈 수 없어요	I can't go outside
날씨가 흐리지만 따뜻해요	The weather is cloudy but warm

II. Conversation

A: 오늘 날씨가 어때요?   How is the weather today?

B: 맑지만 바람이 많이 불어요.   It's clear, but very windy.

A: 산책할 수 있을까요?   Do you think I can go for a walk?

B: 바람이 세지만 밖에 나갈 수 있어요. 우산을 가져가세요.   The wind is strong, but you can go outside. Take an umbrella.

A: 알겠습니다. 감사합니다!   Got it. Thank you!

III. Grammar

1. Ability and Inability: -(으)ㄹ 수 있다/없다 (Can/Can't)

-(으)ㄹ 수 있다 is used to express that something can be done, while -(으)ㄹ 수 없다 indicates inability.

How to Use

Verb stem + -(으)ㄹ 수 있다/없다

Eg: 밖에 나갈 수 없어요 (I can't go outside)

Examples

i. 날씨가 좋아서 산책을 할 수 있어요.

ii. 너무 더워서 밖에 있을 수 없어요.

iii. 비가 와서 운동을 할 수 없어요.

iv. 날씨가 추우면 스키를 탈 수 있어요.

v. 화창한 날에 산책할 수 있어요.

2. Conditions for Actions: -(으)려면

-(으)려면 is used to indicate a condition for an action, meaning "if you want to" or "if you intend to."

How to Use

Verb stem + -(으)려면

Eg: 산책을 하려면 날씨가 좋아야 해요 (If you want to take a walk, the weather must be nice)

Examples

i. 등산을 하려면 날씨가 맑아야 해요.

ii. 밖에 나가려면 우산을 가져가야 해요.

iii. 해변에 가려면 날씨가 따뜻해야 해요.

iv. 캠핑을 하려면 비가 오지 않아야 해요.

v. 소풍을 가려면 날씨가 좋아야 해요.

3. Contrasting Ideas: -지만 (But/Although)

-지만 is used to connect contrasting ideas, meaning "but" or "although."

How to Use

Verb/Adjective stem + -지만

Eg: 날씨가 춥지만 재미있어요 (The weather is cold, but it's fun)

Examples

i. 오늘은 맑지만 바람이 많이 불어요.

ii. 날씨가 덥지만 해변에 가고 싶어요.

iii. 바람이 불지만 산책을 할 거예요.

iv. 날씨가 흐리지만 덥지 않아요.

v. 비가 오지만 산책할 수 있어요.

IV. Exercise

1. Fill in the Blanks with -(으)ㄹ 수 있다/없다

i. 오늘은 비가 많이 와서 산책을 _____.

ii. 날씨가 좋아서 공원에서 피크닉을 _____.

iii. 눈이 와서 스키를 _____.

iv. 태풍이 와서 바깥에 _____.

v. 바람이 세서 우산을 잘 쓸 _____.

2. Translate each sentence into Korean using -지만.

i. It's hot, but I want to go outside.

Answer: _____

ii. The weather is cold, but the sky is clear.

Answer: _____

iii. It's raining, but I still want to go for a walk.

Answer: _____

iv. It's foggy, but not cold.

Answer: _____

3. Match each weather situation in Column A with the most appropriate action or recommendation in Column B.

Column A	Column B
i. 태풍이 올 때	a) 우산을 쓰세요
ii. 날씨가 맑을 때	b) 모자를 쓰세요
iii. 비가 올 때	c) 밖에 나가지 마세요
iv. 눈이 내릴 때	d) 산책을 하세요
v. 더울 때	e) 따뜻하게 입으세요

4. Complete each sentence with the correct weather-related phrase from the options provided.

Options:
- 오늘 날씨가 어때요?
- 기온이 얼마나 돼요?
- 바람이 많이 불어요
- 비가 내릴 것 같아요
- 눈이 올 것 같아요

i. A: _____

  B: 기온이 낮고 흐려요.

ii. A: 이번 주말 날씨가 어때요?

  B: _____. 우산을 준비하세요.

iii. A: 내일 날씨가 어떨까요?

  B: _____. 따뜻하게 입으세요.

iv. A: 오늘 바람이 많이 불어요?

  B: 네, _____. 밖에 나가지 마세요.

v. A: _____?

  B: 오늘은 5도예요.

감사합니다

Thank you

Thank you for choosing our Korean Grammar for Beginners book!

You are now well on your way to learning how to read and speak Korean, and we hope that you enjoyed our Hangul grammar book for beginners.

If you enjoyed learning Korean with us, we would very much like to hear about your progress in a review

We are always eager to learn if there is anything we can do to make our books better for future students. We are committed to making the best language learning content available! Please do get in touch with us via email if you had a problem with any of the content in this book:

hello@polyscholar.com

Visit our website for more books from Jennie and Polyscholar.

Our bestselling book Learn Korean for Beginners focuses on Korean stroke order if that is something you want to learn as well.

POLYSCHOLAR

www.polyscholar.com

APPENDICES

I. Numerals

NATIVE KOREAN NUMBERS

1 - 하나	One	30 - 서른	Thirty
2 - 둘	Two	40 - 마흔	Forty
3 - 셋	Three	50 - 쉰	Fifty
4 - 넷	Four	60 - 예순	Sixty
5 - 다섯	Five	70 - 일흔	Seventy
6 - 여섯	Six	80 - 여든	Eighty
7 - 일곱	Seven	90 - 아흔	Ninety
8 - 여덟	Eight		
9 - 아홉	Nine		
10 - 열	Ten		
11 - 열하나	Eleven		
12 - 열둘	Twelve		
13 - 열셋	Thirteen		
14 - 열넷	Fourteen		
15 - 열다섯	Fifteen		
16 - 열여섯	Sixteen		
17 - 열일곱	Seventeen		
18 - 열여덟	Eighteen		
19 - 열아홉	Nineteen		
20 - 스물	Twenty		

SINO-KOREAN NUMBERS

일	One
이	Two
삼	Three
사	Four
오	Five
육	Six
칠	Seven
팔	Eight
구	Nine
십	Ten
백	Hundred
천	Thousand
만	Ten Thousand
십만	Hundred Thousand
백만	One Million
천만	Ten Millions
억	Hundred Millions

II. Expression of Time

1. Parts of the Day

아침	Morning
오전 (AM)	Before noon
오후 (PM)	Afternoon
낮	Daytime
저녁	Evening
밤	Night
새벽	Dawn/early morning

2. Days of the Week

일요일	Sunday
월요일	Monday
화요일	Tuesday
수요일	Wednesday
목요일	Thursday
금요일	Friday
토요일	Saturday

3. Time of Day Expressions

지금	Now
곧	Soon
이따가	Later (Today)
나중에	Later (In General)
방금	Just Now
어제	Yesterday
오늘	Today
내일	Tomorrow
모레	The day after tomorrow
그제/그저께	The day before yesterday

4. Months of the Year

일월	January	칠월	July
이월	February	팔월	August
삼월	March	구월	September
사월	April	시월	October
오월	May	십일월	November
유월	June	십이월	December

4. Days of the month

1일	1st	21일	21st
2일	2nd	22일	22nd
3일	3rd	23일	23rd
4일	4th	24일	24th
5일	5th	25일	25th
6일	6th	26일	26th
7일	7th	27일	27th
8일	8th	28일	28th
9일	9th	29일	29th
10일	10th	30일	30th
11일	11th	31일	31st
12일	12th		
13일	13th		
14일	14th		
15일	15th		
16일	16th		
17일	17th		
18일	18th		
19일	19th		
20일	20th		

III. Counter Suffixes

1. General Counter Suffixes

Counter	Used For	Example
개	General objects	사과 두 개
명	People	학생 세 명
마리	Animals	개 한 마리
권	Books	책 다섯 권
장	Flat objects (paper)	종이 세 장
병	Bottles	물 네 병
잔	Cups, glasses	커피 한 잔
대	Vehicles, machines	차 두 대
송이	Flowers, clusters	꽃 세 송이
그루	Trees	나무 두 그루

2. Counters for Currency and Units

Counter	Used For	Example
원	Korean currency	오백 원
번	Times, occurrences	한 번
층	Floors	삼 층
쌍	Pairs (e.g., shoes)	신발 한 쌍
박스	Boxes	우유 두 박스
인분	Servings of food	삼 인분

3. Counters for Time and Age

Counter	Used For	Example
시간	Hours (duration)	두 시간
분	Minutes	십 분
초	Seconds	삼십 초
일	Days	사 일
달	Months (Native)	세 달
개월	Months (Sino-Korean)	오 개월
년	Years	일 년
살	Age	열 살

Answer Keys

Chapter 1

1.
  i. 는
  ii. 은
  iii. 는
  iv. 은
  v. 는

2.
  i. **A.** 이름이 뭐예요?, **B.** 안녕하세요
  ii. **A.** 선생님, **B.** 반갑습니다
  iii. **A.** 미국, **B.** 한국 사람
  iv. **A.** 직원, **B.** 학생

3.
  i. 인도
  ii. 중국
  iii. 일본
  iv. 태국
  v. 인도네시아

4.
  i. 학생
  ii. 입니다
  iii. 실례합니다
  iv. 김 선생님
  v. 만나서

Chapter 2

1.
  i. 을
  ii. 를
  iii. 를
  iv. 를
  v. 을

2.
  i. 읽어요
  ii. 공부해요
  iii. 봐요
  iv. 좋아해요
  v. 해요

3.
  i. 저는 신문을 안 읽어요
  ii. 저는 영어를 공부 안 해요
  iii. 저는 잡지를 안 봐요
  iv. 저는 일을 안 해요
  v. 저는 영화를 안 좋아해요

4.
  i. 책 - d. Book
  ii. 사전 - e. Dictionary
  iii. 잡지 - a. Magazine
  iv. 신문 - b. Newspaper
  v. 한국어 - c. Korean language

5.
  i. 잡지
  ii. 안 읽어요
  iii. 책
  iv. 공부 안 해요
  v. 볼펜과 연필

Chapter 3

1. i. 이
ii. 이
iii. 의
iv. 에

2. i. 지갑이 사무실에 있어요.
ii. 거울이 화장실에 있어요.
iii. 가족 사진이 집에 있어요.
iv. 이불이 빨래방에 있어요.

3. i. 가방이 편의점에 있어요.
ii. 거울이 화장실에 있어요.
iii. 지갑이 사무실에 있어요.
iv. 이불이 집에 있어요.

4. i. c) 집의
ii. b) 화장실에
iii. a) 가방이
iv. a) 식당이

5. i. Cosmetics - f. 화장품
ii. Restaurant - c. 식당
iii. Pillows - a. 베개
iv. Mart - e. 마트
v. House - d. 집
vi. Bag - b. 가방

Chapter 4

1. i. 노트북이에요
ii. 도서관이에요
iii. 공원이에요
iv. 의사예요
v. 냉장고예요

2. i. 냉장고가 거실에 있어요.
ii. 친구가 공원에 가요.
iii. 선생님이 학교에 없어요.
iv. 동생이 도서관에 와요.
v. 사진이 벽에 있어요.

3. i. b) 병원
ii. a) 학원
iii. b) 은행
iv. a) 공원
v. c) 교회

4. i. 카메라예요
ii. 선생님이에요
iii. 도서관이에요
iv. 텔레비전이에요
v. 은행이에요

5. i. b) 도서관
ii. c) 책
iii. b) 카페
iv. a) 네, 있어요
v. a) 맞아요
vi. 침대, 소파

Chapter 5

1. i. 시
   ii. 시
   iii. 반
   iv. 십오 분
   v. 시

2. i. b
   ii. e
   iii. a
   iv. c
   v. d

3. i. 세 시 십오 분
   ii. (next Wednesday's date)
   iii. 월요일
   iv. (next year's day of the week for May 10)
   v. 토요일

4. i. 읽고 있어요
   ii. 보고 있어요
   iii. 하고 있어요
   iv. 놀고 있어요
   v. 산책하고 있어요

5. i. 가족
   ii. 일요일
   iii. 혼자
   iv. 기차
   v. 친구

Chapter 6

1. i. 가족
   ii. 친구
   iii. 동생
   iv. 직원
   v. 학생

2. i. 예쁘고, 친절하세요
   ii. 크고, 멋있어요
   iii. 부지런하고, 조용하세요
   iv. 날씬하고, 활발하세요
   v. 크고, 똑똑하세요

3. i. 형은 크고 멋있어요
   ii. 어머니는 예쁘고 요리를 절하세요.
   iii. 여동생은 날씬하고 활발하세요
   iv. 아버지는 크고 똑똑하세요

4. i. 가족이 몇 명이에요?
   ii. 형은 키가 크고, 멋있어요.
   iii. 어머니는 어떤 분이세요?
   iv. 친구가 세 명 있어요.
   v. 여동생은 날씬하고 활발하세요.

5. i. b) 다섯 명
   ii. b) 키가 크고, 부지런하세요
   iii. a) 친절하시고, 얌전하세요
   iv. b) 날씬하고, 활발해요
   v. c) 서울

Chapter 7

i. 읽으세요
ii. 마시세요
iii. 청소하세요
iv. 오세요
v. 보내세요

2. i. e
   ii. c
   iii. a
   iv. b
   v. d

3. i. 기다려 주시겠어요?
   ii. 앉아 주시겠어요?
   iii. 도와 주시겠어요?
   iv. 열어 주시겠어요?

4. i. 저를 도와주시겠어요?
ii. 문을 닫아 주세요.
iii. 잠깐만 기다려 주시겠어요?
iv. 이거 사 주세요.
v. 커피를 만들어 주시겠어요?

5. i. 물 좀 주세요
ii. 저를 도와 주시겠어요?
iii. 창문을 열어 주세요
iv. 여기 앉으세요
v. 잠깐만 기다려 주세요

Chapter 8

i. 뭐
ii. 어디
iii. 언제
iv. 누구
v. 어떤
vi. 언제

2. i. b
ii. a
iii. c
iv. d

3. i. 지금 뭐 먹어요?
ii. 지금 누구에게 전화해요?
iii. 친구 어디에서 일해요?
iv. 버스는 언제 도착해요?
v. 오늘은 왜 늦어요?

4. i. 영화를 볼까요?
ii. 지금 밥을 먹을까요?
iii. 주말에 산책 갈까요?
iv. 내일 어디 갈까요?
v. 같이 커피를 마실까요?

5. i. 배우고
ii. 끝나요
iii. 받았어요
iv. 타고
v. 보내

Chapter 9

i. 마시고
ii. 하고
iii. 만나고
iv. 보내고
v. 먹고

2. i. b
ii. c
iii. a
iv. e
v. d

3. i. 마시고
ii. 좋아해요
iii. 싫어해요
iv. 좋아해요
v. 가고

4. i. 저는 공원에 가고 싶어요.
ii. 그녀는 차를 마시는 것을 좋아해요.
iii. 그는 운동을 싫어해요.
iv. 텔레비전을 보고 싶어요?
v. 저는 책 읽는 것을 좋아해요.

Chapter 10

i. 하려고 해요: 여행을 하려고 해요
ii. 좋아해요: 운동을 좋아해요
iii. 중요해요: 건강이 중요해요
iv. 재미없어요: 영화가 재미없어요

2.
i. c   vi. g
ii. a   vii. f
iii. b   viii. e
iv. h   ix. j
v. d   x. i

3.
i. 청소하는 것
ii. 조깅하는 것
iii. 책 읽는 것
iv. 그림 그리는 것
v. 달리는 것

4.
i. 즐겨요
ii. 중요해요
iii. 좋아해요
iv. 할 수 있어요
v. 중요해요
vi. 하려고 해요

5.
i. 자전거 타는 것을 즐겨요.
ii. 요리하는 것이 중요해요.
iii. 축구하는 것은 재미있어요.
iv. 나는 수영을 배우려고 해요.
v. 요가는 쉽지 않아요

Chapter 11

i. 만났어요
ii. 산책했어요
iii. 이사했어요
iv. 봤어요
v. 읽었어요

2.
i. 여행해 본 적 있어요
ii. 먹어 본 적 있어요
iii. 가 본 적 있어요
iv. 쳐 본 적 있어요
v. 타 본 적 있어요

3.
i. 저는 어제 서울에 갔어요
ii. 지난밤에 친구와 영화를 봤어요
iii. 저는 주말에 친구를 만났어요
iv. 저는 어제 저녁을 요리했어요
v. 저는 아침에 책을 읽었어요

4.
i. c
ii. e
iii. b
iv. a
v. d

5.
i. 여행했어요
ii. 전시회에서
iii. 먹었어요
iv. 먹어 본 적 있어요
v. 읽었어요
vi. 전에

Chapter 12

i. 입학할 거예요봐요
ii. 볼 거예요
iii. 갈 거예요
iv. 읽을 거예요
v. 할 거예요

2.
i. 공부하려고 해요
ii. 요리하려고 해요
iii. 이사하려고 해요
iv. 여행하려고 해요
v. 만나려고 해요

3.
i. 떠날 것 같아요
ii. 합격할 것 같아요
iii. 올 것 같아요
iv. 만날 것 같아요

4. i. 아침에 운동을 할 거예요.
   ii. 이번 주말에 친구를 만날 거예요.
   iii. 오늘 저녁에 비빔밥을 먹을 거예요.
   iv. 다음 주부터 시험을 준비할 거예요.
   v. 주말에 영화를 볼 거예요.

5. i. 저는 다음 달에 공부를 시작할 거예요.
   ii. 우리는 이번 주말에 축제에 갈 것 같아요.
   iii. 저는 내년에 서울로 이사하려고 해요.
   iv. 아마 내일 친구를 방문할 거예요.
   v. 그녀는 6월에 졸업할 것 같아요.

Chapter 13

i. 보다 더
ii. 보다 더
iii. 보다 더
iv. 보다 더
v. 더

2. i. b
   ii. d
   iii. e
   iv. c
   v. a

3. i. 저는 일보다 휴식을 더 좋아해요
   ii. 저는 맥주보다 와인을 더 좋아해요
   iii. 저는 책보다 영화를 더 좋아해요
   iv. 저는 신발보다 옷을 더 좋아해요

4. i. 보다 더 편안해요
   ii. 보다, 좋아해요
   iii. 가장 빠릅니다
   iv. 보다 더 비싸요
   v. 보다 덜 피곤해요

5. i. 이 영화가 가장 재미있어요
   ii. 저는 버스보다 차를 더 좋아해요
   iii. 이 커피가 저 커피보다 덜 달아요
   iv. 이 가방이 모든 가방 중에서 가장 비싸요

Chapter 14

i. 기뻐요
ii. 슬퍼요
iii. 화가 나요
iv. 기뻐요
v. 슬퍼요

2. i. 좋은 소식을 들어서 기뻐요.
   ii. 그녀는 슬퍼서 울고 있어요.
   iii. 그는 지금 화를 내고 있어요.
   iv. 저는 행복하고 싶어요.
   v. 친구가 떠나서 슬퍼요.

3. i. 슬퍼요 - b
   ii. 기뻐요 - a
   iii. 화나요 - c
   iv. 놀라요 - d
   v. 행복해요 - e

4. i. 저는 지금 울고 있어요.
   ii. 그녀는 화를 내고 있어요.
   iii. 아이가 놀라고 있어요.
   iv. 우리는 지금 행복해하고 있어요.

5. i. 좋은 소식을 들어서 기뻐요
   ii. 일이 잘 안 돼서 슬퍼요
   iii. 저는 행복하고 싶어요
   iv. 그는 지금 웃고 있어요
   v. 차가 막혀서 화나요

Chapter 15

i. 일어나야
ii. 요리해야
iii. 끝내야
iv. 운동해야
v. 봐야

2. i. 일찍 일어나는
ii. 양치질 하는
iii. 읽는
iv. 자는
v. 하는

3. i. 방을 청소할 필요가 있어요
ii. 더 공부할 필요가 있어요
iii. 이메일을 확인할 필요가 있어요
iv. 내일의 회의를 준비할 필요가 있어요
v. 건강을 위해 운동할 필요가 있어요

4. i. b
ii. a
iii. d
iv. c
v. e

5. A. i. 세수
ii. 운동
iii. 이메일
iv. 저녁
v. 책

B. i. False
ii. True
iii. False
iv. True
v. False

Chapter 16

i. 운동
ii. 날씨
iii. 긴장
iv. 가방
v. 화학 제품

2. i. b) 팔꿈치
ii. a) 발목
iii. c) 팔
iv. c) 배
v. b) 다리

3. i. 피부가 가려워요 - b
ii. 허리가 아파요 - d
iii. 다리가 아파요 - c
iv. 눈이 아파요 - a
v. 손목이 아파요 - e

4. i. 두통 때문에 병원에 가야 해요.
ii. 컴퓨터 작업 때문에 손목과
손가락이 아파요.
iii. 저는 매일 아침 공원에서 운동을 해요.
친구도 같이 와요.
iv. 무거운 물건을 들어서 허리가 아파요.
v. 책을 읽어서 눈도 피곤해요.

5. i. 운동을 많이 해서
ii. 공원에서
iii. 병원에 가서 진료 받기
iv. 무릎
v. 집에 있고 싶어 해요

Chapter 17

i. 와서
ii. 추워서
iii. 불어서
iv. 맑아서
v. 더워서

2. i. c) 춥다
ii. b) 좋다
iii. b) 따뜻하다
iv. a) 설렌다
v. b) 덥다

3. i. 덥네요
ii. 시원하네요
iii. 많네요
iv. 오네요
v. 맑네요

4. 봄이 겨울보다 더 따뜻해요.
저는 비 오는 날보다 맑은 날이 더 좋아요.
오늘 날씨가 어제보다 더 시원해요.
여름이 가을보다 더 더워요.
맑은 하늘이 구름 낀 하늘보다 더 좋아요.

5. i. 맑은 날 - a
ii. 비 오는 날 - e
iii. 더운 여름 - d
iv. 눈 내리는 겨울 - b
v. 바람이 부는 가을 - c

Chapter 18

i. 볼 때
ii. 읽을 때
iii. 할 때
iv. 할 때
v. 먹을 때

2. i. a) 운동하러
ii. c) 러
iii. a) 낚시하러
iv. b) 찾으러
v. c) 러

3 A. i. 저는 음악을 들을 때 편안해요.
ii. 친구와 테니스를 칠 때 재미있어요.
iii. 요리할 때 저는 항상 레시피를 봐요.

B. i. 저는 운동하러 헬스장에 갔어요.
ii. 친구와 같이 자전거 타러 공원에 갔어요.
iii. 산책하러 공원에 갔어요.

C. i. 저는 독서하면서 음악을 들어요.
ii. 친구와 산책하면서 이야기해요.
iii. 요리하면서 새로운 레시피를 생각해요.

Chapter 19

i. 갈 거예요
ii. 있을 거예요
iii. 방문할 거예요
iv. 할 거예요
v. 먹을 거예요

2. i. 서울에 갈 때는 한복을 c
ii. 제주도에 가면 흑돼지를 f
iii. 유명한 관광지라서 미리 e
iv. 친구와 함께 경주에 h
v. 한옥에서 자보는 것이 d
vi. 관광지에서 지도를 b
vii. 해운대 해수욕장에서 수영을 g
viii. 남산에서 야경을 a

3. i. 부산
    ii. 수영을 하고 싶어요
    iii. 회
    iv. 해운대 해수욕장
    v. 숙소를 예약하는 것

4. i. 저는 다음 주에 한옥에서 묵을 거예요.
    ii. 친구와 같이 서울타워에 가는 게 좋다.
    iii. 경복궁에서 전통 옷을 입어 보고 싶어요.
    iv. 제주도에서 바다를 봐 보고 싶어요.
    v. 여행할 때 미리 예약할 거예요.
    vi. 전주 한옥마을에 가보는 게 좋다.

Chapter 20

i. 에서
ii. 까지
iii. 나
iv. 이나
v. 에서

2. i. 서울에서 부산까지 - b
    ii. 공항에서 호텔까지 - c
    iii. 전철이나 - e
    iv. 교통이 복잡할 때는 - d
    v. 서울에서는 버스나 - a

3. i. 세 시간 동안 기차로 갈 거예요
    ii. 집에서 회사까지 버스나 지하철을 타요
    iii. 45분 동안 택시를 타고 갔어요
    iv. 버스를 타거나 걸어서 갈 수 있어요
    v. 공원에서 집까지 자전거를 타고 산책을 했어요

4. i. 고속열차
    ii. 약 두 시간 반
    iii. 택시나 버스
    iv. 버스
    v. 하루 동안

Chapter 21

i. 개
ii. 명
iii. 병
iv. 마리
v. 권

2. i. 물 - c
    ii. 치킨 - a
    iii. 사람 - b
    iv. 수박 - e
    v. 잡지 - d

3. i. a) 개
    ii. a) 명
    iii. b) 병
    iv. c) 권
    v. a) 마리

4. i. 사과 세 개 주세요.
    ii. 물 네 병 얼마예요?
    iii. 친구 다섯 명 만났어요.
    iv. 치킨 한 마리 좀 깎아 주세요.
    v. 책 네 권 읽었어요.
    vi. 수박 세 개 주세요.

Chapter 22

i. 하기로 **2. i. c)** **3.** i. 친구를 초대할까요? **4. i. b**
ii. 만날까요 **ii. a)** ii. 이번 주에 약속을 정할까요? ii. a
iii. 만날까요 **iii. c)** iii. 저는 준비가 됐는데, 당신은요? iii. e
iv. 할까요 **iv. b)** iv. 이번 주에 생일 파티를 열까요? iv. d
v. 축하하기로 **v. c)** v. 친구들과 기념일을 축하할까요? v. c

Chapter 23

i. 안 돼요 **2.** i. 담배를 피우면 안 돼요 **3.** i. e
ii. 하니까 ii. 위험하니까 조심하세요 ii. c
iii. 들어가면 iii. 지정된 장소에 버려야 해요 iii. a
iv. 하면 안 돼요 iv. 소리를 내면 안 돼요 iv. d
v. 해요 v. b

4. i. 도서관에서 음식을 먹으면 안 돼요.
ii. 병원이니까 소리를 내면 안 돼요.
iii. 출입 금지 구역에 들어가면 안 돼요.
iv. 영화관에서 휴대폰을 사용하면 안 돼요.
v. 여기에 주차하면 안 돼요.

Chapter 24

i. 계세요 **2.** i. a) 인사해야 **3.** i. 지켜야
ii. 가세요 ii. b) 지켜야 ii. 배려해야
iii. 보세요 iii. c) 배려해야 iii. 지켜야
iv. 가셨어요 iv. a) 지켜야 iv. 존경해야
v. 하셨어요 v. b) 양보해야 v. 조용히 해야

4. i. 나이 - b) 연세 **5.** i. 할머니께서 조심하라고 하셨어요.
ii. 이름 - a) 성함 ii. 어머니께서 잘 먹으라고 하셨어요.
iii. 집 - e) 댁 iii. 선생님께서 내일 뵙겠다고 하셨어요.
iv. 밥 - d) 진지 iv. 어른들께 자리를 양보해야 해요.
v. 아프다 - c) 편찮으시다 v. 아버님께서 출장 가신다고 하셨어요.

Chapter 25

　i. 하면서
　ii. 들으면서
　iii. 풀면서
　iv. 읽으면서
　v. 하면서

2. i. a) 읽기 쉬워요
　ii. b) 풀기 어려워요
　iii. b) 외우기 쉬워요
　iv. b) 완성하기 어려워요
　v. b) 이해하기 어려워요

4. i. 수업을 들으면서 - c
　ii. 시험을 준비하기 위해서 - a
　iii. 　공부하면서 - e
　iv. 　예습을 하면 - b
　v. 장학금을 받기 위해서 - d

5. i. 저는 공부를 하면서 음악을 들어요.
　ii. 교과서를 읽으면서 복습을 해요.
　iii. 강의를 들으면서 필기를 정리해요.
　iv. 친구와 문제를 풀면서 질문을 해요.
　v. 저는 수업을 들으면서 노트를 정리해요.

Chapter 26

　i. 후에
　ii. 후에
　iii. 　후에
　iv. 　후에
　v. 후에

2. i. 마세요
　ii. 마세요
　iii. 마세요
　iv. 마세요
　v. 마세요

3. i. 쉬는 게 좋아요
　ii. 마시는 게 좋아요
　iii. 자는 게 좋아요
　iv. 있는 게 좋아요
　v. 가는 게 좋아요

4. i. 두통이 있을 때 - d
　ii. 열이 높을 때 - c
　iii. 　목이 아플 때 - a
　iv. 　피곤할 때 - b
　v. 배가 아플 때 - e

5. i. 두통이 / 게 좋다
　ii. 게 좋다
　iii. 게 좋다
　iv. 후에
　v. 기침이
　vi. 두통이 / 마세요
　vii. 식사 / 후에
　viii. 목이 / 마세요

Chapter 27

i. c   2.   i. 알려주세요   3.   i. 2층에 가면 화장실이 있습니까?
ii. e   ii. 있습니까   ii. 출구가 어디에 있는지 알려 주세요.
iii. b   iii. 있습니다   iii. 1층에 약국이 있습니까?
iv. a   iv. 나옵니다   iv. 엘리베이터는 입구 근처에 있습니다.
v. d   v. 있습니까   v. 3층에 도착한 후에 왼쪽으로 도세요.

4.   i. a) 입구   5.   i. 건너편에 있어요
    ii. a) 사거리   ii. 오른쪽으로 도세요
    iii. c) 건너편   iii. 왼쪽에 있어요
    iv. b) 입구   iv. 계단을 내려가세요
    v. b) 코너   v. 옆에 있어요

Chapter 28

i. 잔액을 확인해 주세요   2.   i. a
ii. 번호표를 뽑으세요   ii. b
iii. 체크카드를 발급해 주세요   iii. b
iv. 비밀번호를 입력하세요   iv. a
v. 통장을 정리해 주세요   v. b

3.   i. 번호표를 뽑고 기다리면 돼요.   4.   i. c
    ii. 비밀번호를 입력하면 출금할 수 있어요.   ii. b
    iii. 신분증을 가지고 있으면 계좌를 만들 수 있어요.   iii. d
    iv. 키패드를 누르면 돼요.   iv. e
    v. 통장을 제출하면 잔액을 확인할 수 있어요.   v. a

Chapter 29

i. 요금   2.   i. a   3.   i. 수신인 주소를 정확히 적어야 해요.
ii. 특급   ii. c   ii. 소포를 받으려면 신분증을 가져야 해요.
iii. 송장   iii. b   iii. 발송비를 지불해야 해요.
iv. 서명   iv. a   iv. 소포를 안전하게 포장해야 해요.
v. 우체국   v. b   v. 상태를 확인하려면 송장 번호를 확인해야 해요.

4. i. **d)** 송장을 다시 요청하십시오
   ii. **a)** 요금을 지불하십시오
   iii. **c)** 등기 우편으로 보내십시오
   iv. **e)** 특급으로 발송해 주세요
   v. **b)** 직원에게 문의하십시오

Chapter 30

i. 못 해요
ii. 할 수 있어요
iii. 탈 수 있어요
iv. 나갈 수 없어요
v. 수 없어요

2. i. 덥지만 밖에 나가고 싶어요.
   ii. 날씨가 춥지만 하늘은 맑아요.
   iii. 비가 오지만 산책하고 싶어요.
   iv. 안개가 있지만 춥지 않아요.
   v. 화창하지만 바람이 많이 불어요.

3. i. 태풍이 올 때 - **c)** 밖에 나가지 마세요
   ii. 날씨가 맑을 때 - **d)** 산책을 하세요
   iii. 비가 올 때 - **a)** 우산을 쓰세요
   iv. 눈이 내릴 때 - **e)** 따뜻하게 입으세요
   v. 더울 때 - **b)** 모자를 쓰세요

4. i. 오늘 날씨가 어때요?
   ii. 비가 내릴 것 같아요
   iii. 눈이 올 것 같아요
   iv. 바람이 많이 불어요
   v. 기온이 얼마나 돼요?